paint alchemy

annie sloan

paint alchemy

recipes for making and adapting your own paint
for home decorating

COLLINS & BROWN

First published in Great Britain in 2001 by
Collins & Brown Limited
London House, Great Eastern Wharf,
Parkgate Road, London SW11 4NQ

1 2 3 4 5 6 7 8 9

Always handle poisonous and corrosive chemicals with care. Follow the
manufacturer's instructions; store chemicals in a secure place, out of the
reach of children and in clearly marked, non-food containers.
Information advice and statements made in this book with regard
to methods and techniques are believed to be true and accurate.
however, neither the author, copyright holder nor publisher can
accept legal liability for omissions.

British Library Cataloguing-in-Publication Data:
A catalogue record for this book is available from the British Library

ISBN 1-85585-886-X

PROJECT EDITOR: Emma Callery
DESIGNER: Luise Roberts
PHOTOGRAPHY: Tino Tedaldi
EDITORIAL ASSISTANT: Niamh Hatton

Reproduction by Classic Scan Pte Ltd., Singapore
Printed and bound byTat Wei Printing PTE Ltd., Singapore

Distributed in the United States and Canada by
Sterling Publishing Co, 387 Park Avenue South, New York,
NY 10016,USA

Contents

The desire to decorate our walls, furniture and even ourselves has caused people to be very inventive and seek out all sorts of coloured materials and sticky substances to make paint. Out of almost nothing, people have found things to paint with. Prisoners during the Second World War used make-up and charcoal to make paint. In South Africa, the Ndebele people in the townships decorate their walls with a black substance found in discarded car batteries. Paint can be made using simply the ingredients from a well-stocked kitchen. The spice turmeric powder provides a good yellow. Mix it with yoghurt, egg yolk or flour paste and

Introduction

in no time you have a paint. The ancient alchemists were really early chemists and had a hand in making and developing the first pigments. Imagine the power of these brilliant colours and how they would have been such a valuable resource for trading. Even today, some pigments are highly valued commodities.

Piles of brilliant and subtly coloured pigments are the real inspiration for making paint. The breadth of colours available is breathtaking and I defy anyone to not feel stimulated by a shop well stocked with pigments. The direct and vital quality of the colours is enough to make your heart strings zing. The usual reaction is that you can't wait to get your hands on them and start making paint. I hope you feel the same about this book.

What is paint?

At its simplest, paint is pigment and glue. To make it fluid, water or the appropriate solvent such as turpentine in an oil paint or methylated spirit in shellac varnish is added. One characteristic of paint is that it adheres to and sits on the surface, unlike a stain, which penetrates the surface.

Pigment ...

The pigment is the colouring matter and can be anything that is capable of making a colour. It is a fine powder suspended in the binder. Traditionally, the most easily available pigments were the coloured earths. There is a whole gamut of browns, reds, oranges, yellows and even green soils that are sifted and ground to powder ready to be added to paint. Some plants provide colour, too, such as indigo, turmeric and burnt wood in the form of charcoal. Nowadays, most pigments are synthetically made for permanence and strength, although many of the earth colours are still used as they are readily available and strong *(see also Pigments, overleaf).*

... + glue ...

In paint, the glue is the sticky part that binds the colouring matter and also allows it to adhere to wood, paper, plaster or fabric. For this reason, the glue is usually called the binder. Types of binder are tremendously varied and give each paint its own particular character. The binder you choose determines whether the paint has a glossy or matt finish and whether or not the paint is durable. Gelatine, for instance, is a weak binder, making it perfect if you want a paint that can be washed off, whereas PVA is very strong but has a shiny finish. Many of the binders used in the past were discovered by resourceful and inventive practitioners using readily available materials that were cheap and plentiful *(see also Binders on page 22).*

... = paint

Paint is basically very simple and can be made at the kitchen table using products in the cupboard or from your local hardware counter. This book shows you how to do it.

Pigments

Pigments are simply the colouring matter for paints, waxes and varnishes. They are very fine powders and hang as tiny particles in suspension in a binder to make the colour and so form paint. The best analogy for them is spices – they have varying strengths and their own characteristics. Some pigments are opaque, others mix well in oil and others are better in water, while some have a granular quality. They fall into four broad areas: pigments from the earth, synthetic pigments and those derived from plants and dyes. To avoid confusion over descriptive colours, all pigment names in this book start with capital letters.

Pigments from the earth
Certain areas of the world present us with earths that are sieved, ground or crushed to result in both mellow and vibrant colours – the ochres, siennas and umbers of the pigment world. Some of these are used almost directly from the ground while others are heated to make the colours darker or redder (Burnt Umber and Burnt Sienna, for example). There are also rare and more difficult to obtain splendid colours from stones such as Malachite, Azurite, Lapis Lazuli and Cinnabar. However, these are now obsolete or used for restoration purposes as they are so expensive.

Synthetic pigments
A synthetic pigment sounds like it is a modern product. In fact, pigments have been manufactured since early times. Nowadays there are many modern synthetic pigments, which are very popular as they are strong and reliable. Many have complicated, unfriendly chemical names such as Pyranthrone Orange, Irgazine Ruby or Indanthrone Blue, which has led companiesto invent their own names and combine them into their own favourites and then call them by an entirely new name. To add to the confusion, some modern pigment names have made their way into the pigment vocabulary, such as Hansa Yellow, Quindo Red, Alizarin Crimson and Phthalocyanine Green.

Pigments from plants
Roots, berries, flowers and bark provide us with some beautiful colours. Some of these colours are of historical interest only, such as reds made from madder root. Others are still used today. Blues are made from powdered indigo root; turmeric and saffron make glowing golden yellow (see page 66) and the sap of iris flowers makes a lovely green for delicate work on paper (although it fades quickly when exposed to direct light). Real cochineal, made from the dried bodies of a Mexican insect, makes a beautiful pink colour.

Pigments from dyes
A dye is like a stain in that it impregnates fabric or paper rather than sticking to the surface like paint. Dyes can be used as pigments but they first have to be added to an inert pigment – a pigment with no colour, such as chalk. Traditionally, these dyes were called lakes and are made from organic sources like madder root.

Source your pigments from everywhere. Raid the kitchen for turmeric and real cochineal or use powder pigments or universal stainers from a decorator's supplier.

Universal stainers tend to be more difficult to control than pigments, come in a narrow range of colours and are generally less inspiring.

Pigment names and strengths

There is no standard for pigment names and their strength. They can be mixed with extenders to make them go further so it is impossible to give precise quantities for the recipes given in this book. Instead, the recipes should be used as a guideline for how much pigment I used to create the colour shown on the page. Any name can be given to a pigment, even a well-known traditional name such as Yellow Ochre. A pigment with this name may have been dug from the earth but equally it may be a synthetic Mars Yellow.

In this book, my criteria for choosing pigments are safety, cheapness and strength. On the following pages I outline the most commonly available pigments, grouped by colour. Of these, my suggested starter palette is given on page 26.

HANDLING PIGMENTS AND PAINTS

Always take care when handling pigments. Only a few pigments are known to be poisonous and these are no longer available for purchase, but to be on the safe side follow this advice.

- Always wear a face mask and work in a well-ventilated room to avoid inhaling the powder.
- Wear a barrier cream or wear gloves and wash your hands after handling pigments.
- Dedicate an old refrigerator to storing any of the animal-based paint recipes given in this book (see page 46, 61, 62, 70, 72 and 80). Never store these products in a refrigerator used to store food.
- Keep all dyes and chemicals in a safe dry place away from cooking areas and out of reach of children and pets.

Yellow pigments

The range of yellows is relatively small compared to that of reds or blues. The yellow pigments fall into two distinct categories – natural and artificial. The naturals are those from the earth – the ochres and siennas – and provide many very beautiful and useful yellows. Their exact hue depends on where in the world the pigments come from, such as France, Italy or the USA. The amount of iron oxide and manganese present in the pigment also affects the colour, making greenish yellows through orange and pinkish tones. These are the colours of buildings in Venice, Naples and Casablanca and are wonderful for interiors as they are so warm and mellow. These are the backbone of the yellows as they make some of the most easy-to-live-with tones. The pigments appear dark and brownish in dry powder form but once mixed in a binder they become bright, yet soft and mellow. Nowadays, synthetic iron oxides, sometimes called Mars colours, are used as they are cheap and strong.

The artificial or manufactured yellows tend to be bright and sharp. The traditional ones, Cadmium, Chrome and Cobalt Yellow, tend to be used by artists rather than decorators as they are expensive and toxic. Cadmium is thought to be a carcinogen but is still available (although banned in California); Chrome Yellow is unavailable as it is carcinogenic and lead-based, and Cobalt Yellow is expensive. Various synthetic yellows such as Hansa Yellow or Azo have taken their place as they are cheap and reliable.

There are many pigments with names such as primrose, sun or buttercup that describe a colour. It is usually not possible to know what the actual pigment is but it is likely to be a synthetic pigment mixed with a very pale or colourless extender to make the pigment inexpensive.

EARTH ORANGE

This orange comes from mixing together several earths to make this bright but earthy tinged orange. There are other synthetic oranges on the market but they often lack the depth and subtlety of the earth tones.

YELLOW OCHRE

A light, mellow, mustard-coloured ochre, which is a natural earth found all over the world (the best grades come from France) and used from earliest time. Yellow Ochre gets its colour from iron oxide.

It can now be artificially produced from Mars Yellow.

RAW SIENNA

The darkest of all the yellows, this is a transparent type of ochre made of natural iron oxide of weak strength. The colour varies enormously from an earthy yellow to a brownish gold, but is always mellow and warm. Mars Yellow can also replace this colour.

CADMIUM YELLOW

Cadmium makes many strong yellows, from lemon through to

EARTH ORANGE

EARTH ORANGE
AND WATER

YELLOW OCHRE

YELLOW OCHRE AND
WATER

RAW SIENNA

RAW SIENNA AND
WATER

CADMIUM YELLOW

CADMIUM YELLOW
AND WATER

CADMIUM LEMON

CADMIUM LEMON
AND WATER

HANSA YELLOW

HANSA YELLOW AND
WATER

orange. Because of its toxicity many synthetic yellows are taking its place, but Cadmium remains one of the strongest, truest yellows available. When mixing a yellow with blue to make green (see page 104) use this yellow without any hint of orange in it.

CADMIUM LEMON

There are several lemon yellows, but all lack strength. Cadmium, on the other hand, has good covering power. It is useful for making greens with blues although on its own it can be rather too harsh and acidic, especially for use as a wall colour. Use Cadmium Lemon with Cobalt Green to make a good lime green (see page 101).

HANSA YELLOW

A modern, permanent, semi-transparent, synthetic yellow, which is added to a colourless product to make a pigment. The colour varies but is usually a bright yellow. Hansa Yellow is cheap and replaces the traditional pigments, although the strength is variable.

Red pigments

The range of reds is very wide, from brilliant scarlets, through deep crimsons with tinges of blue, to all the brown-reds and pinks. The red pigments divide neatly down the middle between the earth reds and the artificial reds.

There is a very large range of earths containing red iron oxide that look like warm browns to the uninitiated, but when thinned or with white added beautiful and subtle colours are revealed – brick reds, plum reds and old pinks. To supplement them and to make them less expensive, synthetic iron oxide is manufactured to make a superb range of strong red earth colours. These are called Mars colours. However, part of the joy of pigments is the romantic, evocative names and the subtle qualities of the old pigments. Many have names suggestive of exotic places where they have been sourced in the past. Indian Red and Caput Mortuum (meaning 'dead head' in Latin due to the way the pigment forms skull shapes as it is mixed), are both bluish reds, which turn to a beautiful shade of bluish pink when white is added.

Other red oxides have more of an orange bias, such as English Red, also known as light red. For truly bright reds the Cadmiums are essential, although there are concerns that these are carcinogens. There are also many synthetic alternatives available including some bright pinks. Alizarin Crimson is a firm favourite, making a rich cherry red and, with white, a slightly mauve bright pink. However, this can fade if used with white or in a glaze over a white ground. A good replacement is the synthetic Quindo Red.

CADMIUM VERMILLION HUE

This is a red nearer the orange part of the spectrum, popularly called strawberry or scarlet red. True Vermillion is very expensive and is largely replaced by either Cadmium Red Orange or a synthetic pigment of the same colour.

CADMIUM RED

This comes in a variety of shades from a deep dark red, as here, to a bright almost orange red. It is banned in California as it is deemed carcinogenic. There are several similar synthetic reds available that are permanent and strong, called Chinese Red, Signal Red, Studio or Permanent Red.

ALIZARIN CRIMSON

A very strong red pigment with a bluish tone making ruby, burgundy and blood reds. With white, brilliant magenta pinks can be made. The discovery of how to make this pigment in the nineteenth century was a big breakthrough, overtaking the need for pigments and dyes from the madder plant. It is strong, permanent and transparent.

VENETIAN RED

This is a manufactured iron oxide with additives to imitate an original red clay pigment. Mars Red is the name for the pure iron oxides that are made nowadays. Other iron oxide mixtures imitating old colours are English or Light Red, a scarlet earth colour making a good warm pink when white is added. Indian Red, Spanish Red and Dead Head Red make beautiful violet-tinged pinks.

BURNT SIENNA

This is a very useful brown-red earth pigment, almost as useful as Raw Umber (see page 21) as it can be used to tone down greens and blues. It can vary from ginger red to warm brown. It is a form of Raw Sienna, roasted at high temperatures to change its colour from yellow to red. It is slightly transparent.

RED OCHRE

This is a pure red earth or clay. This particular one comes from France, where some of the finest earth pigments come from, being very clear and intense in tone (see Yellow Ochre page 12).

CADMIUM VERMILLION HUE

CADMIUM VERMILLION AND WATER

CADMIUM RED

CADMIUM RED AND WATER

ALIZARIN CRIMSON

ALIZARIN CRIMSON AND WATER

VENETIAN RED

VENETIAN RED AND WATER

BURNT SIENNA

BURNT SIENNA AND WATER

RED OCHRE

RED OCHRE AND WATER

Blue and violet pigments

There are no blue earth pigments, making it a unique characteristic of all these colours. Compared to the ease of digging yellows, oranges and reds almost straight out of the ground, obtaining blue has always been a complicated process. For this reason, the colour blue was for centuries highly prized and thought to be special. The clothes of the Madonna and special figures in medieval paintings were often painted in blue to signify their distinctive nature. As a primary colour, blue pigments are valuable for making greens and purples.

The original blues – Lapis Lazuli, Azurite and Smalt – have all been superseded by alternatives, although they are still used in restoration work. From plants, indigo root was used principally as a fabric dye but also as a watercolour paint. Today, Ultramarine, Phthalocyanine Blue and Cobalt Blue are the major blue pigments. Ultramarine is one of the most adaptable of all the pigments as it can be made into many blues, from deep reddish shades to green-tinged blues. Phthalocyanine, also known as Heliogen Blue, is used increasingly as it can be manufactured in all the shades of blue. The blues are mainly strong transparent or semi-transparent colours and so are easy to use.

The range of blues is huge, covering violet and lavender blues through grey blue, navy, royal and sky blue to all the greenish shades of teal, turquoise and aquamarins. As a result, mixing blues to make other colours can be tricky as there are so many of them and their tonal qualities vary so much. A warm blue will have an undertone of red so if this is used to make a green, a brownish muddy colour will result. In the same way, Prussian Blue contains hints of green so do not use it to make a purple as the end result will not be a clean colour (see also page 104).

PRUSSIAN BLUE

PRUSSIAN BLUE AND WATER

COBALT BLUE

COBALT BLUE AND WATER

TURQUOISE BLUE

TURQUOISE BLUE AND WATER

PRUSSIAN BLUE

This is a very powerful pigment that looks almost black in powder form. When mixed with water the blue is cool and slightly greenish. With white added the blue is a clear cool blue. It is very useful for making greens with the addition of yellow (see page 104). Some varieties, Paris and Milori, are specifically for oil or water. Nowadays, Prussian Blue is likely to be made from an artificial Phthalo Blue pigment.

COBALT BLUE

This is a good blue mid-way between the warmth of Ultramarine and the coolness of Prussian Blue. It is more expensive than Ultramarine so is used more by artists rather than decorators and is useful as a limeproof pigment (see page 30).

TURQUOISE BLUE

There are no natural turquoise pigments but there are various Cobalts, Ultramarines and Phthalocyanine Blues that can be used. Phthalocyanine is an extremely strong synthetic organic pigment manufactured to resemble blue.

ULTRAMARINE

This is the workhorse of the blues as it is cheap, strong and can be used in many binders, including some in lime and cement. One of the reasons for its popularity is that it makes a warm blue and it looks so appealing in powder form – very bright and intense.

ULTRAMARINE VIOLET

A useful violet-blue pigment making a good twin for the Manganese Violet described below. There are various synthetic violet pigments, some reddish and others bluish, which can also be used (see Manganese Violet).

MANGANESE VIOLET

It is not entirely necessary to have a violet as a pigment as the colour can be mixed from Alizarin Crimson and Ultramarine with white, but for consistency if using a lot of the colour and to obtain the subtlety of this colour, then this is a good pigment. It is permanent and reasonably strong.

ULTRAMARINE

ULTRAMARINE AND WATER

ULTRAMARINE VIOLET

ULTRAMARINE VIOLET AND WATER

MANGANESE VIOLET

MANGANESE VIOLET AND WATER

Green pigments

Considering the wide range of shades the term green encompasses – lime green, turquoise, grass green and all the grey greens – there are relatively few green pigments. It has always been hard to make greens that are strong and permanent. In fact, many historical greens, such as Verdigris, blacken with time. Emerald Green had the added disadvantage of being poisonous – it was once used as an insecticide. In many old paintings the trees seem to be painted black but, in fact, they are just blackened greens. Conversely, plant greens like Sap Green fade with time. This may be why green has a reputation for being unlucky with some people.

The most commonly used green pigments for interior decorating are Cobalt Green, Oxide of Chromium and the spectacularly named and important Phthalocyanine (or Phthalo, for short) Green, otherwise known as Heliogen Green. The latter is the most important green pigment as, with the addition of other pigments, it can be used to make so many different greens. Any bright light greens can be made from this with yellow and possibly white added (*see page 107 for other ways of using green*). Many greens are made by mixing blue and yellow. There is only one green earth pigment, Terre Verte, and this is not really green, more a grey with a faint celadon tinge.

TERRE VERTE
Also known as green earth, this is a popular colour despite being low in strength and covering power. True Terre Verte is a grey with just a hint of green, but through the naming of artists' paints the colour has come to mean a sage green. As a result, various greens are added to the natural green earth to make a pigment of the expected greenness, as shown here.

OXIDE OF CHROMIUM
This is a very good earthy sage green with a hint of yellow. It is a good substitute for an earth green as it is opaque and does not fade, although it is not very strong.

COBALT GREEN
A mellow, slightly blue middle green, to be used just as it is. To further the range of Cobalt Green, add Titanium White to make aquamarines and duck-egg blues.

TERRE VERTE **TERRE VERTE AND WATER**

OXIDE OF CHROMIUM **OXIDE OF CHROMIUM AND WATER**

COBALT GREEN **COBALT GREEN AND WATER**

VIRIDIAN **VIRIDIAN AND WATER**

PHTHALOCYANINE GREEN **PHTHALOCYANINE GREEN AND WATER**

VIRIDIAN

Viridian is a transparent and strong bright green that is similar to Phthalo Green (see right) but more subdued and without much blue in it. It is less harsh than Phthalo Green.

PHTHALOCYANINE GREEN

When this green, sometimes known as Heliogen Green, was introduced in 1938 it immediately became very popular as it was cheap and opened up lots of new possibilities, particularly when mixed with white. The resulting shades of spearmint green, aquarmarine and Nile green, as well as the more intense turquoise greens, became especially popular for interior decorating. Phthalocyanine Green is a copper-based green and it is extremely reliable, permanent, intense and strong. But to give it more character add a little blue or Burnt Sienna.

Black, brown and white pigments

There is not just one black, one brown and one white but several, making this twilight corner of the pigments full of subtlety and interest. The blacks are either blue or brownish in colour, the browns are green or pinkish and the whites milky or snowy.

The blacks were made from earliest times from carbon. Powdered grape-vine charcoal and burnt animal bones make a bluish black, and from soot a brown black can be obtained, provided a tiny amount of white is added. Avoid using black to tone down or darken colours as it tends to muddy them. Use umbers instead, or add a little of the colour's complementary (*see page 96*). Synthetic Black Iron Oxide is now used predominantly as it is extremely cheap and very strong.

There are many browns, most in the red or yellow earth category, but Raw and Burnt Umber make perfect neutral colours, especially when white is added (*see page 96*). The umbers are also useful for toning down other colours. Raw Umber and white make a very beautiful neutral that is useful on woodwork and as a backdrop for brightly coloured furniture and fabrics.

White always brings out the true nature and underlining character of a pigment, so it is probably the most important of all the pigments. Chalk can be used as a pigment, although it is no use in oil paints and is not powerful. Nowadays, though, Titanium White is used predominantly because it is opaque and very white.

TITANIUM WHITE

TITANIUM WHITE AND WATER

LAMP BLACK

LAMP BLACK AND WATER

BONE BLACK

BONE BLACK AND WATER

RAW UMBER

RAW UMBER AND WATER

BURNT UMBER

BURNT UMBER AND WATER

TITANIUM WHITE

This white, in use since about the 1920s, was the first really opaque pigment with good covering power, making possible the fashion for white interiors. Add Titanium White to a binder with another pigment colour and it renders the paint opaque.

LAMP BLACK

Originally made by using the powdery soot from a fire, this makes a brownish black. These days, these blacks are likely to be made from synthetic iron oxide and known as Mars Black.

BONE BLACK

Originally made by burning ivory chips, and sometimes called Bone, Vine, Lamp or Carbon Black, the name is used to describe a bluish black that is particularly apparent when mixed with white. One of my favourite colours is achieved by adding a little black to lemon yellow to create a lovely olive green. These days, these blacks are also likely to be made from synthetic iron oxide and known as Mars Black.

RAW UMBER

A cool brown with a faintly greenish tinge, becoming a delightful grey brown when white is added, makes Raw Umber a perfect foil for any colour. This is a very useful colour for toning down too bright a colour without using black (see page 96).

BURNT UMBER

This is an earth pigment made by burning raw umber. It makes a dark chocolate colour and with white added the colour has a slight pinkish tone depending on the exact type and quality.

Binders

The binder is the glue that sticks the pigment to the surface. It is also sometimes called the medium. Without it, the pigment would simply run and not stick to the surface. Furthermore, it is the binder that characterizes the paint, giving it its particular texture and strength. The name of the paint is usually the name of the binder, hence oil paint is pigment bound in oil, glue paint is pigment bound in glue and so on. The major attribute a binder must have is transparency, so that the colour of the pigment will not be influenced. It must also be able to stick to a particular surface and be able to dry.

The popular modern commercial water-based paints in home decorating use acrylic or vinyl resin as a binder. All the more interesting materials have been sidelined into the artists' camp, but even there a preponderance of acrylic-based paint can be found. This results in a certain similarity in our paints. However, by using basic, readily available materials, a wide variety of paints can be made. Many of the binders used in ancient and classical fimes, such as gum, egg and glue, have remained unchanged throughout the centuries and remain valid.

Basic materials

The basic materials can be categorized into three areas – binders from animals, those from plants and those from the earth. Animals supply a huge variety of materials, including eggs, milk (casein), skins (gelatine and size) and beeswax. Shellac used for making lacquer is made from a resinous secretion from an insect. From plants we get gums (gum arabic), resins, oils, wax and starch (flour). The earth provides us with all the ingredients for plasters and cements, such as marble dust and lime, the latter being one of the most important ingredients of paint. From the earth we also obtain acrylics and vinyls via the oil industry and these make up the bulk of binders for modern paints.

Choosing your binder

When selecting which binder to use it is a good idea to ask yourself various questions. Is this a large area? Do you want a shiny or matt surface? Are you able to buy specialist materials? Do you want a quick result? Are you concerned with using traditional environmentally friendly materials? If you have a large area to paint, don't mind a slightly shiny finish and you want to do it cheaply and without specialist materials, then you might choose a PVA binder.

All the binders from the kitchen are accessible, particularly flour for a starch paint (*see page 68*) and eggs (*see pages 65 and 66*). You may also want to choose your binder from an environmental standpoint. Again, the kitchen-cupboard binders fit the bill, as do old materials such as limewash, polished plaster and gesso (*see pages 50, 52 and 78-81*).

CLOCKWISE, FROM THE TOP: *Factory-made binders are the norm nowadays but binders can be made from a wide range of materials including rabbitskin granules, casein, linseed oil, eggs and lime putty.*

Making paint

There is no specialist equipment needed for making paint as almost everything you need can be improvized from your kitchen cupboards or nearby hardware store. Don't be put off by a long intimidating list of items. Having said that, there is some specialist equipment that would be useful if you are going to become a specialist in a particular area such as lacquer work, where precision and attention to detail are important. Also, it is essential tto wear a face mask when handling pigments, to prevent inhaling the powder (see *Handling pigments and paints on page 11).*

Mixing pigment into solution

Generally, pigment isn't added from its dry state directly into the medium, although for small quantities it is possible, especially where decorative designs are being made with either of the egg paints on pages 65 and 66 for instance.

Avoiding gritty pigments

Sometimes pigments are very gritty and take too long to break down simply by mixing them with a liquid medium. It will speed things up if you start by crushing your pigment to get rid of any large, hard lumps. A gritty pigment can be very annoying if it hasn't been ground out, especially when you are painting small areas. The paint will look as if there is grit or small lumps in it and when you try to wipe them off the surface you get pigment bursts, resulting in a spotty surface. Pigment bursts that happen when the paint is wet can be attractive when they are in large areas to give a hand-made look. But there should not be so many that the true colour cannot be controlled.

In small areas of paint, a burst of pigment can radically alter the tone of a colour. It is best to test a little of your chosen pigment first to see if it needs any grinding. Once the pigment is added it is also worth leaving your paint to stand for at least an hour. This helps the pigment to disperse more evenly and create a more intense colour.

Preparing pigments for paint

1 Put the pigment on a tray and grind it by rolling over it and pressing down with a certain amount of pressure. Use an old rolling pin or pestle and mortar set aside for the purpose. Traditionally, a slab of marble or glass with a glass muller would be used. Dampen the pigment and grind it on the slab until there are no more lumps.

2 Put the pigment into a container (an old jar, for instance), and mix with a little of the binder you are about to use, e.g. PVA, rabbitskin glue or white paint, until a coloured liquid paste has been achieved without any lumps or flaring from undissolved nuggets of pigment. Pour into the rest of the binder and stir well so it is thoroughly dispersed.

EQUIPMENT FOR MAKING PAINT

For grinding

A tray or piece of smooth wood and an old rolling pin set aside specially for the purpose.

Or a pestle and mortar – steal from the kitchen but remember that once used it cannot be returned to the kitchen as some pigments are poisonous. The best pestle and mortars are made of stone-like material but a wooden one could be used.

For mixing paint

Jars for mixing small quantities.

Sticks or old paint brushes to stir large quantities

Small brushes for small quantities.

Buckets, basins or plastic paint kettles for large quantities.

Paper towel or rags to keep your work area and tools clean.

Face mask around your face as the powder can be very fine if you are mixing large quantities of paint.

Specialist materials if you are really getting serious

Muller and slab for grinding your pigments.

Starter palette for interior decoration

When first beginning to make paint it can be overwhelming to see the number of pigments that are available. So to make life more straightforward, here is a set of pigments that I have chosen to make a good range of colours across the spectrum. Two reds, a blue and a yellow are included, from which secondary and complementary colours can be created (see pages 96-99), and there is also Titanium White and Raw Umber to further the range of shades. From this basic palette of colours, you can then add others to suit yourself. A basic palette is very personal and will vary according to the sort of work you are doing. For example, colours mainly used for decorating interior walls tend to differ from those for painting exterior walls.

The successful mixing of colours depends on experimentation, but always keep the number of pigments used at any one time to a minimum. Pages 91-107 explain how to make the most of pigments to suit any room in your home by adding them to shop-bought paints or creating your own colours.

THE STARTER PALETTE
Starting from the top of the photograph opposite and working in a clockwise direction, the starter kit colours are: Ultramarine, Titanium White, Burnt Sienna, Cadmium Lemon, Prussian Blue and Cadmium Red. Don't feel obliged to stick with these suggestions: Cobalt Blue could be used in place of Ultramarine. Likewise, if you won't need to make many greens or are keen on a more muted range of colours, substitute Yellow Ochre for Cadmium Lemon. Alternative shades for the Cadmium Red would be the pigment Alizarin Crimson or look for a Quindo Red.

ULTRAMARINE
This is a warm and popular blue, especially on its own. When mixed with the deep Cadmium Red, it also allows for purples. For greens, mix Ultramarine with Cadmium Lemon. To make the colour deeper and greyer, add Burnt Sienna and Titanium White.

TITANIUM WHITE
It is absolutely necessary to have white to tone down colours and to make them opaque rather than translucent. Adding just a touch of white to any pigment can bring out its colour all the more, making it brighter and more interesting. Titanium is the most opaque, so is the best.

BURNT SIENNA
This colour helps tone down colours so they lose their brightness in the same way as Raw Umber. Add to greens and blues to make sophisticated greys and blue-greens. Mixed with Titanium White it will also make good terracottas, warm browns, pinks and oranges.

CADMIUM LEMON
By using a lemon yellow rather than an orange yellow, clean greens and turquoises can be made. Start with Cadmium Red and add some Cadmium Lemon for an orange yellow.

PRUSSIAN BLUE
A second blue is necessary if you feel you will be needing a good range of blues to enhance the potential of your colour mixes. Prussian Blue mixed with Cadmium Lemon results in a lovely green and for a deep purple mix it with Cadmium Red. Experiment with different quantities of Titanium White for pale shades of duck egg blue which look elegant in any living room.

CADMIUM RED
A good bright red is necessary and this particular red is useful as it can be used to make purple by adding Ultramrine. Add Titanium White to make a clean, rather sweet, pink and a touch of burnt sienna to make a more complex pink.

RECIPES:
LARGE

QUANTITIES

Coloured varnish

translucent veil

Applying a mixture of varnish and pigment gives a surface colour without obliterating the base. This is a particularly good recipe if you want to cover a wooden floor or wooden furniture so the grain of the wood is still visible. Using white pigment in the varnish gives a bleached wood effect. There are many varnishes available so it is important to use the right one for the job in hand. For a floor needing tough protection, for example, use a floor varnish and apply it with a roller for speed. Once the correct colour has been achieved, the second and subsequent coats can be made using a plain uncoloured varnish.

The recipe here is for a water-based varnish but a coloured oil-based varnish is made in the same way. The floor shown to the left has a varnish made using a grey rather than pure white. To make this, white pigment was used plus a little yellow and violet to make a taupe grey (*see page 96*). Start by adding the main colour to the varnish. In a separate bowl mix the darker pigment into a little varnish until dissolved. Pour a little at a time into the main pot, stirring all the time until the right colour has been achieved. Test on a piece of wood to see the strength of your colour.

Makes 500 ml (18 fl oz) coloured varnish

Ingredients

500 ml (18 fl oz) water-based varnish

1½ tsp pigment (here I used Titanium White)

½ tsp coloured pigment (here I used Hansa Yellow and Ultramarine Violet)

You will need

2 bowls

metal spoon

LEFT: *Two coats of varnish using Titanium White, Hansa Yellow and Ultramarine Violet pigments result in a sophisticated grey.*

Add pigment to floor varnish by first mixing the pigment with a little of the floor varnish and then adding this to the rest of the varnish. If you are mixing two pigments or more, decide which is the main one, work that into the bulk of the varnish, then slowly add a little of the others, testing all the time, until the right colour has been created. Use white pigment only if you want to create an opaque colour.

ABOVE: *A wooden bowl with a decorative grain coated with a green-pigmented varnish. The varnish was allowed to drip down the sides of the bowl and silver bronze powder was sprinkled on.*

PVA paint
a glossy coat

PVA will be familiar to many as a wood glue, a cheap glue used in schools or as a builder's material for sealing walls. It appears white when in its container and when first applied but as it dries it becomes transparent with a shiny finish. The addition of pigment will make it opaque, especially if white is added.

The letters PVA stand for polyvinyl acetate, which basically means that it is a liquid plastic. It is cheap and easily available so it can be used on walls, furniture and on smaller projects. It is also a typical binder in that it can be used in many ways: as a glue, as a paint medium and also as a varnish. PVA is a synthetic version of a traditional resin such as shellac but it is easier to use as it is more practical, being water-based rather than oil-based. It does, however, lack the character of the more traditional resin. Like shellac, it can also be used to make a shiny oriental lacquer.

LEFT: This door with the black surround hints at oriental red lacquer. To create this effect, I added scarlet red pigment to PVA with a little water and applied three coats over a white base (the white helps to give brightness to the red), using a synthetic flat varnish paintbrush. I then brushed out the PVA paint using the tip of a paintbrush to remove as many of the brush strokes as possible. The end result is an uneven finish that has interest and depth.

OPPOSITE: *Yellow Ochre in PVA glue applied over white with a short-haired roller for a delicate texture.*

Makes 1 litre (34 fl oz) PVA paint

Ingredients
1 litre (34 fl oz) PVA glue
1 tbsp pigment (here I used Yellow Ochre) in solution (see page 25)

You will need
2 bowls
metal spoon
paintbrush or stick

Take the PVA glue and, if necessary, add sufficient water to make a runny consistency. Slowly add the pigment in solution, stirring, until you reach your desired colour.

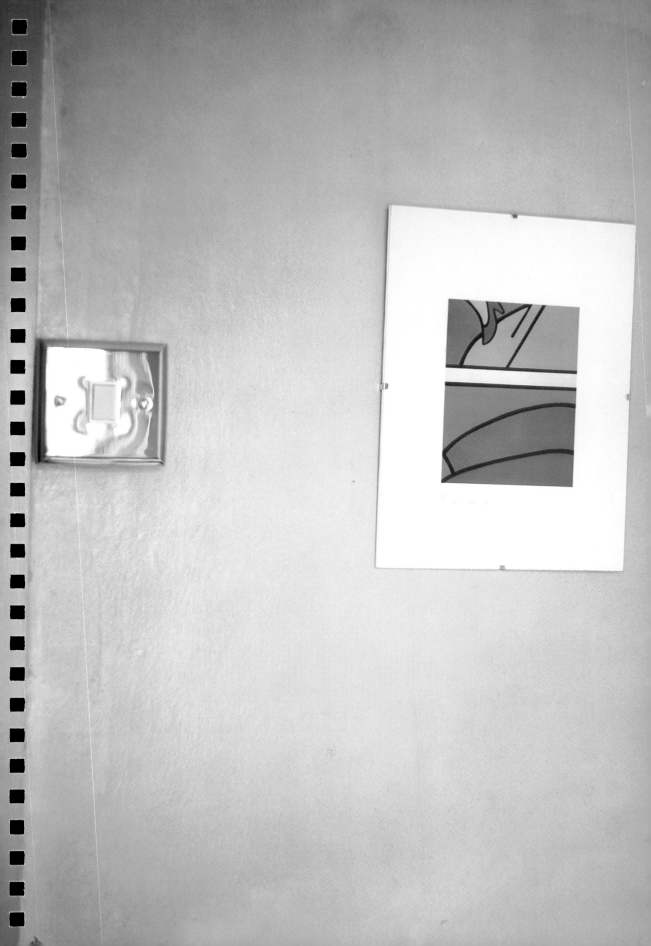

Glitter paint
bright & glistening

Another dimension has been added to the modern paint range with the addition of glitter paints, sometimes called sparkle paints. These paints lie somewhere between a varnish and a paint. Instead of adding pigment to the binder, here large glittery pieces are added. The binder is milky when first applied but it becomes transparent as it dries so both the base colour and the shiny glitter are apparent.

There are several shades of glitters available such as blue, green, red, silver and gold. There are different sizes of glitter too. Here a large glitter is used, which makes a raised texture on the wall.

Once you have made this paint, do not leave the mixture overnight. The dye on the sparkles may leach out and colour the varnish, which might ruin your finished effect.

Makes 500 ml (18 fl oz) glitter paint

Ingredients
500 ml (18 fl oz) water-
   based varnish
3 tbsp large sparkle
   granules (here I used
   emerald and fuchsia
   pink)

You will need
bowl
metal spoon

Spoon the sparkles into the varnish and stir well. When mixed, apply to the surface with a paintbrush. Stir well before each application to ensure an even spread of sparkles.

LEFT: *Sparkle granules can be bought in various sizes to create different degrees of subtlety and density. You can also mix together more than one colour for an even more colourful effect. Here, white and red sparkles have been applied to a burgundy base. In the photograph underneath, red, white and green sparkles to have been mixed in varnish and painted over a Cobalt Blue base.*

OPPOSITE: *Two layers of glitter paint – first emerald and then fuchsia pink – over a bamboo green base.*

Pearl paint
lustrous & silky

To make a pearl paint, instead of a pigment being added to a binder, a flake-like mineral from the earth, called mica, is added. The mica is ground very finely to a talcum powder-like consistency and added to almost any binder to make a shiny, lustrous surface very similar to a pearl shell. The resulting paint catches the light and reflects it so it looks different depending on the light.

There is no need to grind or make up these powders in solution before adding them to your binder. Instead, add them slowly, testing them for colour as you go. Wait for the paint to dry, normally five minutes, before judging the colour. This is important because although pearl powders are available in several colours, each one looks white with only the tiniest hint of a colour. When they are put into a binder, especially a white water-based binder, the colour continues to appear to be white but on drying it is brought out, especially in certain lights.

The base colour to which the paints are applied makes a considerable difference. A dark colour makes the most impact, whereas a pale colour is subtle and delicate.

LEFT: *To achieve a textural effect, paint the base with stripes. Here the stripes are blue and white and the pearl paint has been applied vertically to emphasize the base.*

OPPOSITE: *Blue pearl paint looks bright and luminous brushed over a deep blue base.*

Makes 500 ml (18 fl oz) pearl paint

Ingredients
500 ml (18 fl oz) water-
   based varnish
10 tbsp pearl-lustre
   powder (here I used
   pearl blue)

You will need
bowl
paintbrush

Take the water-based varnish and add the pearl-lustre powder, stirring well.

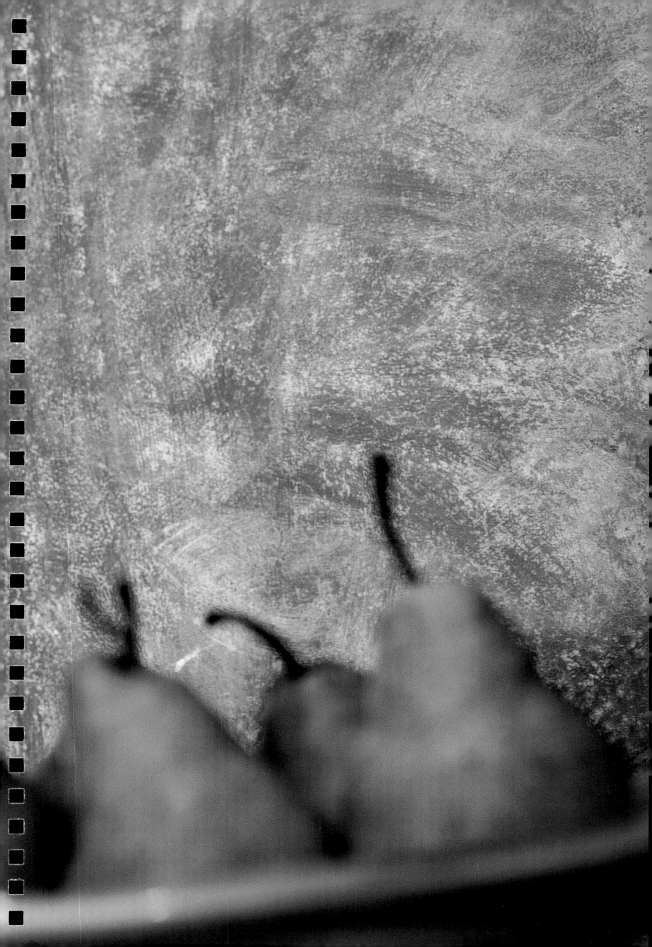

Metallic paint
sleek & shining

Instead of the usual pigments being added to a binder, here metallic powders – called bronze powders – mainly made from very fine brass flakes, are added. There are about ten different coloured metals available, such as a reddish gold and a greenish gold plus some coppers and silvers. They are merely added to a binder of your choice, such as a water-based varnish, as here, or other liquids as diverse as oil, fabric medium or egg white. Used in oil, some of their shine is lost.

Unlike pigments, bronze powders need no grinding or breaking down so they may be added directly to the binder. However, they are even finer than pigments and fly everywhere, so work with a mask. If not enough powder is added, the mixture takes on a faintly purplish hue, which disappears when more powder is added. When bronze paints are applied over a base colour the metallic coat shows in patches. The result is a beautiful variation in hue.

ABOVE: *A wooden bowl has been turned into a luxurious golden bowl with bronze powders.*

Makes 500 ml (18 fl oz) metallic paint

Ingredients
500 ml (18 fl oz) water-
    based varnish
5 tbsp bronze powder
    (here I used gold)

You will need
mask
bowl
paintbrush

Take the water-based varnish and add the bronze powder. Stir until well combined.

OPPOSITE: *Gold-coloured bronze powder applied with a roller over a white base.*

Coloured waxes

mellow sheen

Mixing a clear, colourless wax with pigment is the perfect way to seal a wooden floor or furniture while giving it an interesting colour. Encaustic painting using melted liquid beeswax was a medium from earliest times, but it is used very little now as keeping the wax melted and fluid is tricky. The technique has now been superseded by other paints.

This method with wax uses clear soft furniture wax with pigment, which results in a soft mellow finish with a slight sheen. Any colour pigments can be used, not just the brown of usual furniture waxes, and green, blue or even purple are particularly good colours to enhance your wood.

It is usual to think of wax being applied over wood, but it can also be applied over chalky paint, which absorbs wax well. A brown wax over a blue chalky paint, for instance, gives the paint an aged look. Use a natural wax that contains beeswax or carnauba. There are also water-soluble waxes available.

LEFT: *White pigment has been added to clear wax and rubbed into the open-grained oak wood. The white wax remains in the grain to give the look of limed oak.*

Makes 250 g (9 oz) coloured wax

Ingredients
250 g (9 oz) wax
4 tbsp pigment (here I
   used Viridian)

You will need
plate or shallow container
palette knife
soft wire (steel) wool

LEFT: *Floorboards stained with Viridian pigment blended in wax.*

1 Blend the wax and pigment on a plate or shallow container, making certain that all the pigment is mixed thoroughly.

2 The colour looks very intense when mixed into the wax so test on spare wood. Rub in with soft wire (steel) wool to check it is the desired colour.

Textured paint
gritty texture

Instead of adding pigment to give colour to the paint, here sand is added to give texture – depending on the effect you wish to achieve, you can use any sand from fine to coarse. Together with colour, texture is a most important element in paint. Paints are usually smooth, matt or glossy but this recipe makes a paint with a three-dimensional, rough, gritty finish. This can be used for the effect itself, which has a rustic feel, or to cover a crude or unattractive surface. It can be used over brickwork or to hide textured wallpaper.

The paint needs to have a good body and stickiness to hold the sand. This can be a water-based bought household paint of either matt or satin finish or a paint made using one of the recipes on this book, such as a PVA paint or limewash (*see pages 32 and 50*). The base paint can be white or you may choose to add pigment as well as the sand.

Some of the finer paints in this book would not work with sand added to them. Egg white paint (*see page 66*), for example, will not hold the sand, and for egg yolk paint (*see page 65*) and casein (*see page 62*), there is no point in roughening their finishes. Sand is also added to the lime putty in fresco and it could be used in limewash (*see pages 54 and 50*).

**Makes 1 litre (34 fl oz)
textured paint**

Ingredients
4 tbsp coarse sand
1 litre (34 fl oz) water-
    based household paint
    (here I used white)

You will need
metal spoon
stirring stick

LEFT: *Sand is available in several textures, from coarse with fragments of broken shells to fine white sand.*

OPPOSITE: *Coarse sand added to white bought paint for a rough, textured effect.*

Add the coarse sand tablespoon by tablespoon to the paint, continuously stirring to thoroughly mix in the sand. To change the paint colour, add pigment in solution (*see page 25*). When applying the paint, stir it frequently to prevent the sand from falling to the bottom of the paint pot.

Coloured concrete
gritty smooth

The straightforward grey of cement can have a stark modernity but it can also be enriched by the addition of colour. This can be added by using either dry powdered pigment or by the addition of ready-mixed stainers. Stainers are suggested here because of their strength. Powerful staining is needed to counteract the natural dark colour of the cement. Pigments can be used but some do not react well with cement, weakening its structure (*see page 50*), while others strengthen it. You also require large volumes (up to 10 per cent of the volume of mortar mix that is used), which is expensive. Alternatively, you can subtly colour the concrete by adding quartz powder or chips or sand as well as marble dust.

LEFT: *Sharp sand was used in the making of this mix to give a rough texture on the wall of this house. Yellow Ochre stain was added to make a creamy limestone colour.*

RIGHT: *Ultramarine pigment used to colour and strengthen the cement.*

Makes 2.5 kg (5½ lb) coloured concrete

Ingredients

2.5 kg (5 lb) prepared
    mortar mix
universal stainers (here I
    used Ultramarine)
water

You will need

bucket
trowel
stick
float or trowel

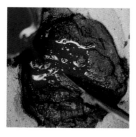

1 Put the prepared mortar into a bucket and mix well to ensure it is evenly distributed. Make a hollow in the dry ingredients.

2 Slowly add stainer to the hollow to make your desired colour. Then add the water, a little at a time and stirring all the time, until a fairly heavy consistency like that of peanut butter is achieved.

3 Apply the mortar with a float or trowel and work it to achieve a smooth flat surface. The colour will appear darker when the mortar is dry.

Distemper (calcimine)
chalky & flat

Distemper (calcimine) is a soft paint that is wonderfully easy to remove, making it the perfect paint for ornate carved or moulded plasterwork – it can simply be washed off before a fresh coat is applied. In addition, its associations with country interiors mean that when used on roughly-hewn walls it gives a distinctive, traditional finish.

It is made from animal glue, whiting and pigment but despite its well established use for colouring mouldings, it can flake, especially when wetted or over painted. To avoid this happening, use a good quality of glue and not too much whiting. Cheap glues like those made from fish bones with a lot of whiting in the mix make a very weak paint.

LEFT: *A cornice painted with a distemper (calcimine) mix ensures the shapes remain crisp – no matter how frequently they are repainted.*

RIGHT: *Raw Sienna pigment in distemper (calcimine) makes a practical matt finish for any wall.*

Makes 1 litre (34 fl oz) distemper (calcimine)

Ingredients
900 ml (30 fl oz) hot water
150 g (5 oz) animal glue such as calfskin or rabbitskin (the finest quality) or pearl glue, the lowest quality
5 kg (11 lb) whiting
6 tbsp pigment (here I used Raw Sienna) in solution (*see page 25*)

You will need
2 bowls
double boiler
whisk(s)
strainer

1 To make the size, pour hot water over the glue granules and allow to soak for three hours or overnight. Then place the whiting in a bowl or bucket, cover it with water, whisk to remove lumps then leave it to soak and sink to the bottom of the bowl, which will take about two hours.

2 Heat the size in a double boiler and whisk it. Do not allow the glue to boil because this can destroy its structure. Pour off the excess liquid from the whiting.

3 Pour the warm size into the whiting through a strainer and then add the pigment. Stir well. Before applying the paint to your chosen surface test it on paper and leave to dry to see the colour. It will usually dry a paler shade. If necessary, add more pigment mixed in solution.

Transparent scumble glaze
clear & deep

A scumble glaze is like a varnish in that it is transparent but it has the added quality of not drying quickly. Traditional glazes are oil-based using linseed oil. Colour is added to the glaze using pigments, and patterns are made in the mixture for such effects as colourwashing, woodgraining and marbling. The base colour remains visible in at least some places.

Nowadays, there are water-based glazes, which are popular as they have no smell and are quick drying. But the traditional oil-based glazes have a distinct advantage in their subtlety. An oil-based glaze is also a more environmentally friendly product than the vinyl and acrylic acetates as the linseed (from flax seed) and turpentine (from pine trees) are all sustainable products. Linseed oil can be bought in the form of boiled or raw. The boiled form dries more quickly than when in its raw state.

Makes 150 ml (5 fl oz) scumble glaze

Ingredients
5 tbsp linseed oil
4 tbsp turpentine
(white/mineral spirit can be substituted)
1 tsp pigment (here I used Dead Head Red)
½ tsp terebine liquid drier (drier)

You will need
bowl
metal spoon

1 Mix together the linseed oil and turpentine, leaving a little of the turpentine to one side.

2 Dissolve the pigment in the remaining turpentine and add to the oil and turpentine mix, a little at a time, until the colour you require is reached. Add the drier, if using.

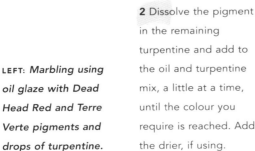

LEFT: *Marbling using oil glaze with Dead Head Red and Terre Verte pigments and drops of turpentine.*

ABOVE: *For a small amount of work, make a water-based glaze by using a water-based varnish and an extender, which retards the drying time.*

Limewash
mellow & matt

Limewash is a simple paint much used in the past and now admired for its matt, chalky texture. It is made from lime putty, water and pigment. Despite its white appearance the lime putty has only a little colour, which benefits from added pigment to provide colour and opaqueness.

In limewash painting, the wall is first wetted with water, or better still with weak lime water, and then the limewash is applied. It is best painted on a porous surface or a traditional lime plaster base. The colour of the wet paint becomes far paler when dry so test a little on paper before going ahead.

Lime is also a constituent of fresco painting (see page 54) and limewash possibly emerged out this technique as pigment is applied over wet lime-bound plaster.

WHICH PIGMENT?

There are some pigments that cannot be used in limewashing, coloured concrete (see page 44), polished plaster (see page 52) or fresco work (see page 54) as they react badly with the very strong alkalinity of the lime in the mortar or react with salts or metals in the atmosphere.

As a general guide, all the iron oxides, which include the Yellow, Orange and Red Ochres plus the blue cobalt pigments (see pages 12, 14 and 16), are perfectly stable. But be wary of Venetian Red as it is an impure mixture of pigments and so can react badly. Also, some of the Ultramarines do not work, although the Ultramarine that I have used here is one of the exceptions. Likewise, copper-based colours do not work in lime.

However, there are also a lot of new synthetic pigments that are limeproof and provide a wide, modern colour range unknown to the early fresco painters. But of these, the Alizarins and some of the very brilliant yellows such as Hansa Yellow cannot be used. It is best to consult a reliable pigment specialist for more specific information. If you are prepared to take the risk and want to experiment with pigment colours, six months' exposure to the atmosphere is usually enough to see whether a pigment is reliable.

Makes 1 litre (34 fl oz) limewash

Ingredients
1 litre (34 fl oz) lime putty
2 tbsp limeproof pigment (see Which pigment? to the left) (here I used Ultramarine)
water

You will need
bowl
stirring stick
paint kettle

OPPOSITE: *For a rich and intense effect of great depth, a second coat of Phthalocyanine Blue limewash was painted over the pale coat given in this recipe.*

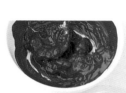

1 Mix the pigment in a small bowl with some water and a little lime putty and stir well until the pigment is all dispersed.

2 Put the remaining lime putty into a paint kettle, or similar large container. Add the pigment and sufficient water to make an easy-flowing liquid. Stir and apply to a wetted wall.

Polished plaster
glossy marble

This is not a paint but a coloured plaster mix which, because of its ingredients and application, has a high shine. It is a very strong material and contains marble dust, which gives it a soft shine. It is also known as Venetian stucco or marmorino and can be applied with variations in the mix to give different textures. There are similarities with fresco (*see overleaf*) as the ingredients are almost the same, but with polished plaster, pigment is added to the mix rather than being painted on the surface.

It is applied in layers, finishing with the finest, which is skimmed to remove the watery excess. The final finish gives it the shine.

LEFT: *A slightly pitted texture was given to this wall by applying a fine-grained finishing coat over a coarser-grained base while the underneath coat was not completely dry.*

RIGHT: *A glorious shine is best achieved with an electric polisher.*

Makes 2 kg (2 lb 4 oz) polished plaster

Ingredients
1 kg (2 lb 4 oz) polished plaster mix or equal amounts of lime, cement, marble dust
water
2 tbsp limeproof pigment (here I used Ultramarine but *see page 50*)
2 tsp shading pigment (here I used Red Ochre)
clear wax (no varnish)

You will need
large container
trowel
stick or electric mixer
float
electric buffer or fine wire (steel) wool and cloth

1 Follow the instructions on the bag of plaster mix or mix the lime, cement and marble dust. Add sufficient water to make a mixture like thick mud, stirring well by hand or with an electric mixer. Add pigment (here, the Red Ochre makes the blue a greyer shade) and stir. Test the colour on a sheet of strong paper and let it dry. The colour will be lighter when dry.

2 Apply two or three layers of the mixture using a float, allowing each to dry or almost dry, depending on the final finish wanted. Leave about 1 hour between coats for drying.

3 To get the polished effect on the final layer, work the float by using it at a steep angle to the wall to remove the water from the plaster mix.

THE FINISHING SHEEN

When the plaster is dry the wall will be softly and unevenly coloured. For a really high shine apply a coat of clear wax and buff with an electric polisher. Or for a more mellow sheen, apply the polish by hand.

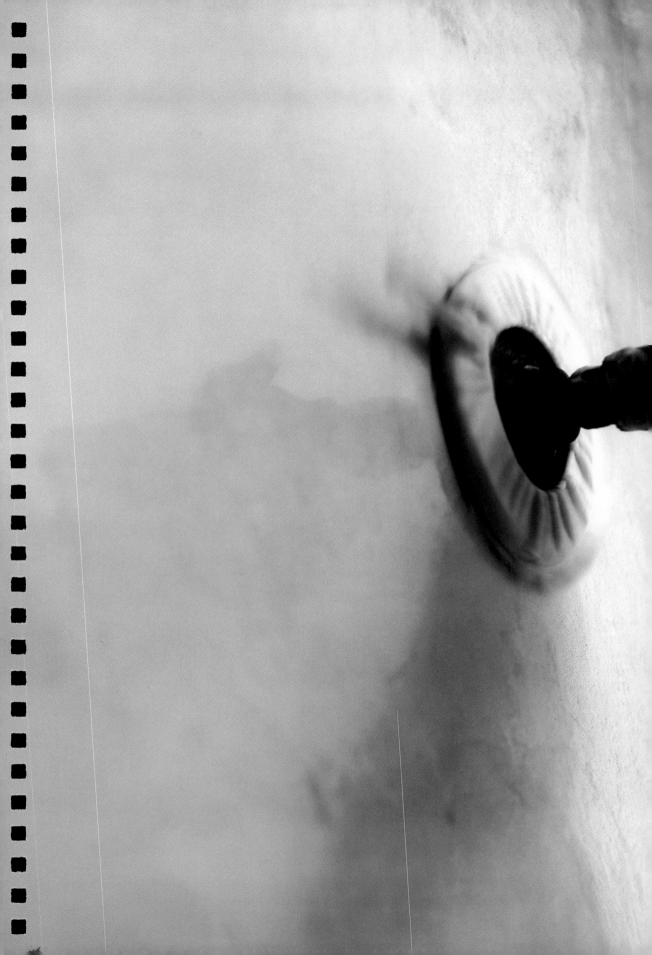

Fresco
indefinable depth

A wall of wet plaster is the binder for the pigment in this recipe. The pigments sink into the wet plaster so the colour is an integral part of the plaster, unlike paint, which sits on the surface. The finished result is colour of great depth, clarity or brilliance, depending on the pigment. This is an ancient technique known not only in Europe but also in Asia. It probably developed from using lime plaster, a very old material, on walls made with coloured earths. Although universal and timeless, the technique has strong historical connections. It was used and developed in Italy, particularly during the Renaissance, and is even today known by its Italian name *buon fresco*, meaning true fresco. A second technique known as *secco fresco*, meaning dry fresco, is where pigments mixed with a binder such as egg, gum or casein are added over the dry plaster.

Three layers of plaster or mortar are needed for fresco. The first one is applied over a lattice of metal or wooden lathes and is roughly textured using coarse sand and lime putty. This is followed by a second coarse layer, called the brown coat, and this is finished off with the final one using equal parts of fine sand and lime putty for a smooth finish to be painted on. Marble dust can be added to the sand (*see polished plaster on page 52*), which adds a sparkled effect.

READY TO PAINT?

The way to check that the final layer of plaster is sufficiently dry for painting (about 1 hour after applying the plaster) is to draw a wet paintbrush across the plaster: if the water is absorbed within a minute, it is ready to paint.

To cover 1 sq m (1 sq yd) make:
For layer 1: 800 g (1 lb 12 oz) plaster
For layers 2 and 3: 1.6 kg (3½ lb) plaster

Ingredients
Layer 1: 3 parts coarse sharp sand to 1 part lime putty
Layer 2: 2 parts coarse sharp sand to 1 part lime putty
Layer 3: 1-1.5 parts fine sharp sand to 1 part lime putty
limeproof pigment powders (*see page 50*) (here, Burnt Sienna and Cobalt Blue were used)

You will need
bucket
round-headed trowel
float
paintbrush

1 Apply the first layer of plaster using the above ratio of sand to lime putty. Leave to dry for 48 hours. Wet the base coat well and apply layer 2, as shown. Leave to dry for 48 hours.

2 Wet the base coat well with water and apply the third layer using the ratios given above. Apply to a maximum thickness of 3 mm (⅛ in), meticulously smoothing it with a float.

3 While damp, paint on the design with pigment mixed with water. The smaller the amount of water added, the more opaque the wash.

RIGHT: *A wash of Cobalt Blue and a band of opaque Burnt Sienna applied to a fresco panel.*

RECIPES:
SMALL

QUANTITIES

Pigment and water
shaker stain

This is an unusual recipe, effective in its simplicity and said to be used by the Shakers in their search for the unadorned life. It is not a true paint as there is no binder and it is really only a method of applying colour to wood. The pigment is mixed with water and heated in a saucepan and the resulting warm wet paste is rubbed into the wood. To help absorption dampen the wood before applying.

The Shakers would have used red and yellow soils straight from the ground and the heating would also have helped kill any bacteria in the soil. The pigment acts like a dye, staining the wood to bring out the grain.

Several applications of the coloured paste may be necessary to get a good depth of colour but after several coats the wood cannot absorb any more and so will just wipe off the surface. Allow each application to dry before painting on the next. Paint is usually a way of protecting wood but by using this recipe only colour is provided so when the wood is dry use wax to seal and protect the surface.

ABOVE: *Rush surfaces absorb a pigment and water mix very well. Finish with a varnish for protection.*

Makes 250 ml (8 fl oz) pigment stain

Ingredients
250 ml (8 fl oz) water
1 tbsp pigment (here I
   used Duck Egg Blue)

You will need
saucepan
metal spoon
rubber gloves
cotton cloth

1 Spoon the pigment into the water in a saucepan. Bring it to the boil and then let it simmer slowly until the water has evaporated, leaving a thickish paste at the bottom of the pan.

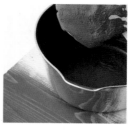

2 Let it cool and then, wearing rubber gloves to protect your hands, soak the cotton cloth in the stain and rub it on to the surface.

RIGHT: *Soft new pinewood absorbs the pigment easily. Here just one coat of pigment paste has been given to this small box.*

Milk paint
simple clarity

Take a carton of milk and let it sour, pour away the watery residue and the result is a very crude but serviceable binder for pigment. It is best to use low-fat milk to make the curds as you then get a larger quantity of binder. To speed up the process, sour milk with lemon juice or start with yoghurt or curd cheese.

This simple paint is not as hard-wearing as casein paint (*see overleaf*) but nevertheless it is efficient and permanent and it has been used since early times, particularly for house painting. Despite being made of milk the paint has no smell and does not go mouldy.

The soured milk will not hold as much pigment as some other mediums such as oil, so the paint won't be opaque. Use white in the mixture to avoid this or paint it on wood so the grain can be partly seen. The curds allow the colour of the pigment to come through very cleanly.

Makes 250 ml (8 fl oz) milk paint

Ingredients
juice of ½ lemon
250 ml (8 fl oz) skimmed milk
2 tsp pigment (here I used Leaf Green) in solution (*see page 25*)

You will need
bowl
sieve
metal spoon

LEFT: *With time, milk paint develops a fine patina, wearing in parts and darkening in others. The paint was applied to the wood and rush.*

FAR RIGHT: *Thick low-fat yoghurt, not the set kind, makes a rich paste just right for using to make paint.*

1 Add the lemon juice to the milk.

2 Leave the milk for several hours in a warm place to curdle. Pour the resulting watery residue (the whey) through a sieve and add the pigment in solution to the remaining curds. Stir well and use.

Casein paint
rich & creamy

Casein is made from milk and is a more sophisticated version of milk paint (*see page 61*). It is bought as a powder that has been made by souring skimmed milk, then washing and drying the curd. The resulting casein powder, which is an acid, is then mixed with another material, an alkali, to make a really strong glue-like binder. The most usual alkalis that are added are lime putty for large areas or ammonium carbonate for smaller decorative areas, as I have used here.

When mixing the paint, take care not to inhale the ammonium carbonate as the smell is quite overpowering. Mixing the simple casein with an alkali is a very good way of making an extremely strong glue as well as a durable paint that has been used for many centuries. The paint dries to a soft matt finish.

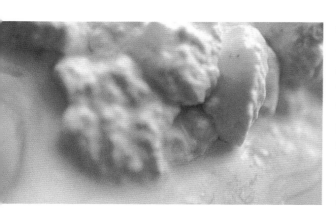

LEFT: *Using 1 part of casein to 4 parts of lime putty makes an excellent, very hard-wearing paint that was popular all over the world for furniture and walls. Soda and borax can also be used as the alkali for the casein.*

RIGHT: *Casein paint has a completely matt finish, as seen on this chair, but it can be polished with a cotton cloth to make a dull sheen. When made properly, casein is the strongest of all paints.*

Makes 250 ml (8 fl oz) casein paint

Ingredients
50 g (2 oz) casein powder
250 ml (8 fl oz) water plus extra for thinning
20–25 g (¾– 1 oz) ammonium carbonate
10 tsp pigment (here I used Terre Verte) in solution (*see page 25*)
2 tsp Titanium White (optional)

You will need
bowl
metal spoon

1 Put the casein powder into a bowl and add the water. Stir well to remove any lumps and make certain the casein is all quite dissolved.

2 Add half of the ammonium carbonate and stir into the mixture. It will effervesce and become slightly sticky. Leave for 30 minutes until it stops fizzing and then add the pigment. Add more water if needed. This paint will keep for a few days.

THE CASEIN TEST

Always test your casein paint before using to see if it flakes. If it does, then there is too much ammonium carbonate, which makes a lot of chalk and causes the paint to flake. Too little ammonium carbonate causes the paint to be powdery and weak.

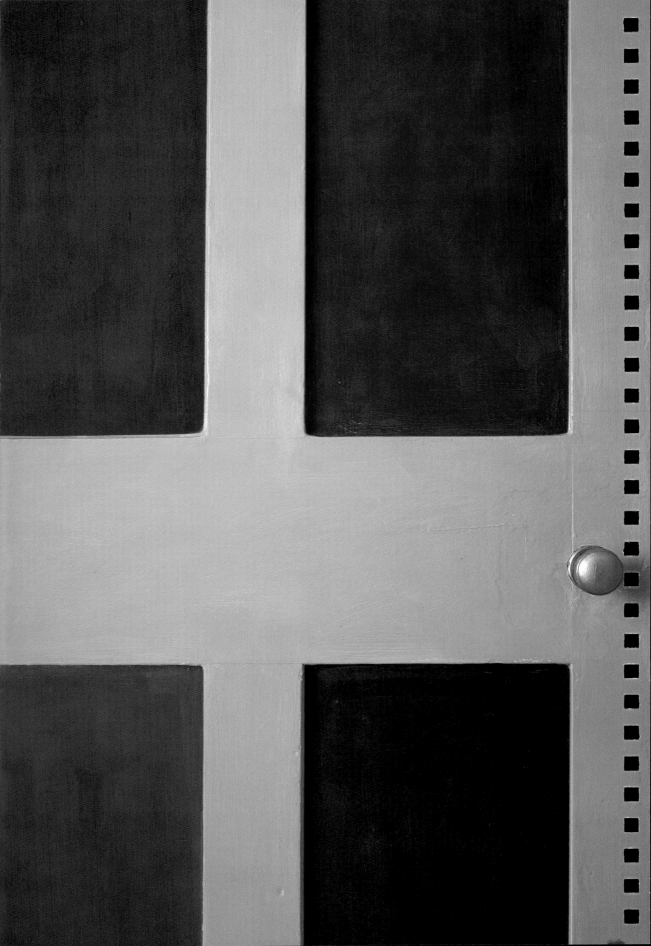

Egg yolk paint

silky smooth finish

'Just add an egg', so the banner goes on packaged cake mixtures. Here it applies to making a paint. Mixing pigment together with egg yolk gives colours a luminous depth and sheen. Interestingly, the colouring agent is not affected by the yolk's colour. This paint is also very strong, as you may know if you have ever left a drop of egg yolk on a plate. It hardens with time, so the longer it remains, the more difficult it is to remove.

The use of egg yolk in paint, often called egg tempera, has a long history. It was commonly used by Flemish artists and by decorative painters in Renaissance Italy. Today, egg yolk paint can be used in many paint effects on walls and furniture. Use soft-haired brushes to apply the paint as bristle brushes destroy its delicate structure.

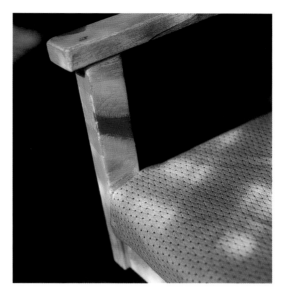

ABOVE: *Egg yolk paint should be translucent to give depth to the colours beneath. Use over a chalky base for the best results.*

Makes 30 ml (1 fl oz) egg yolk paint

Ingredients
1 egg yolk
¼ tsp pigment (here I used Red Ochre)
a little water

You will need
bowl or tray
metal spoon
paintbrush

LEFT: *A larder door in Red Ochre (top right), Yellow Ochre (bottom left) and Fresco Violet with Raw Umber (top left and bottom right).*

1 Separate the yolk, discarding the white or retaining to make egg white paint (*see overleaf*). Remove the outer membrane by pinching the sac. To make this easier to remove, dry the yolk by leaving it for 30 minutes.

2 Add pigment, a little at a time, to the yolk and mix well with a paintbrush. Adding a little water will make it flow properly.

3 Add more pigment to enrich the colour, but not more than a teaspoon as it will then not bind properly. The balance of yolk, pigment and water is important. Test by applying a coat on a sheet of glass. When dry it should peel off in a long continuous film.

Egg white paint
illuminator's colours

The clarity, delicacy and strength of the colours in medieval illuminated manuscripts are stunning. These colours were achieved using white of egg, otherwise known as glair, mixed with pigment or dyes from plants.

Egg white has been known as both a binder for paint and as a delicate glue for gold leaf over gesso for many centuries. The egg white binder has little body and is therefore not a robust paint for woodwork or walls. Rather, it is a paint that works well on paper or fine fabric. Medieval recipes for making glair suggest that the egg white should be whipped into a white froth. Then it should be left to stand until a liquid forms and it is the liquid that is the glair. I used the egg white straight from the egg, but you could also use powdered egg white.

Makes 30 ml (1 fl oz) egg white paint

Ingredients

1 egg white

1 tsp pigment (here I used Cadmium Vermillion Hue)

You will need

bowl

fork

Separate the yolk and white of an egg and put the yolk to one side, perhaps to be used for making egg yolk paint (see page 65). With a fork, whisk the egg white and add pigment. Some water may help the consistency.

ABOVE: *Some of the colours in medieval manuscripts are plant dyes, many of which fade in daylight, but being in books the colours have been protected. You can still purchase some of these plant dyes and they are rather satisfying to use. One such is saffron,* available from a good supermarket or delicatessen. To use saffron in paint, soak the dried saffron in a little egg white for about half an hour and then use on paper to get an intense warm sunflower yellow. Other plants that can be used are the dried petals of the safflower for a red, a green from iris petals and sap green from buckthorn berries. However, each of these fades in light.

RIGHT: *Simple shapes in bright colours on a fine fabric lampshade in contrast to the complex patterns found on illuminated manuscripts.*

Starch paint
simple & light

Many people will remember making glue as children by mixing flour and water and heating it until it forms a sticky glue. Add pigment to this and the result is a crude paint. It is the starch in the flour that makes it sticky. It can be used to make a cheap paint for theatrical painting or other impermanent painting. It should be remembered that a little flour goes a long way so this is probably one of the cheapest forms of paint available.

Some flours contain more starch than others; rice flour, for example, is 75 per cent starch. Other starches that can be used are corn, rice, wheat and, to a lesser extent, potato. Every culture has their own starch and it is often used in the making of arts and crafts, usually as a glue, but in West Africa starch is made from yams and used as a resist in dying the traditional indigo fabrics.

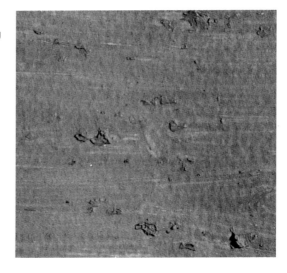

ABOVE: *In Finland, a traditional paint used for the outside of houses involves cooking oats for several hours to bring out the sticky gluten in them. Red and Yellow Ochre are the traditional colours of this interesting mixture.*

STARCH GOUACHE

A more sophisticated form of flour paint contains dextrin, which is available from specialist stores and is made by roasting starch at a high temperature. Mixed with water, this makes a particularly strong glue or paint binder. Dextrin is used for making some gouache paint (*see gum arabic paint on page 74*).

Makes 250 ml (8 fl oz) starch paint

Ingredients
1½ tbsp flour
250 ml (8 fl oz) water
2 tsp pigment (here I used Hansa Yellow) in solution (*see page 25*)

You will need
saucepan
metal spoon

1 Put the flour into the saucepan and slowly add most of the water. Cook the mixture until the water is absorbed. Then slowly add the remaining water, stirring all the time. After all the water has been used to help bring out all the gluten, simmer it over a low heat for about 15 minutes.

2 Take the pan off the heat and then slowly add the pigment in solution, stirring well to bring out the full colour.

RIGHT: *A papier-mâché bowl painted with bright yellow starch paint made from flour.*

Gelatine paint
clear sheen

Here is a kitchen cupboard staple, along with milk, eggs and flour, that can be pressed into service as a paint. Animal gelatine is a weaker form of rabbitskin glue (*see page 22*) being made of bones rather than skin. There are vegetable alternatives made from seaweeds, such as carrageen or agar agar, which work in a similar way to the traditional animal product.

Gelatine has been used as a glue in the past but here it is used as a binder for paint.

An interesting way to use it is on glass, either on a window or under a glass table. This paint is not permanent and, indeed, it will come off when you want to clean the glass. But as gelatine paint is very easy and quick to make, melting when hot water is poured on to it and becoming jelly-like when it cools, you can add a fresh design to your window whenever you like. Like glue size (derived from rabbitskin granules), it needs to be used while it is warm.

Makes 60 ml (2 fl oz) gelatine paint

Ingredients
1 tbsp gelatine powder
60 ml (2 fl oz) hot water
2 tsp pigment (here I used Earth Orange) in solution (*see page 25*)

You will need
2 bowls, one larger than the other
metal spoon
paintbrush

LEFT: *On this window I first chose to paint vertical stripes in various colours of pigment mixed into gelatine. Once dry, I painted horizontal lines using different colours to make a tartan pattern – a third colour is created where the paints overlap.*

Empty a packet of gelatine into a bowl and pour hot water on it, following the instructions on the packet. Once made, keep the mixture warm in its bowl by resting it in a larger bowl filled with hot water. To keep the gelatine liquid, only decant as much gelatine as you need to add the pigment to. It turns to a jelly-like consistency all too quickly.

RIGHT: *Frame a window with two freehand lines of orange and turquoise blue.*

Glue paint
clear & light

This paint works particularly well on wood, which is why it was traditionally used in northern Europe, where wood was used in abundance in houses. It has a translucent quality, giving depth to whatever colour is mixed into the binder. There are a lot of modern glues available, but the one specifically referred to here is traditional rabbitskin glue made, just as it suggests, from the skins of rabbits. Many of the old glues are made from animal products such as skin and bones of fish, calves or lambs. Glue paint is an easy recipe to make but takes a bit of forward planning so that it is ready on the day you need it – the rabbitskin needs to soak overnight.

Once made, the glue can be kept for a few days in a refrigerator in a screw-top jar. If you are storing it with pigment added, stir well before applying. The glue does have a very pungent odour, which at first is disquieting.

ABOVE: *There are various cheap paper glues, often clear brown in colour, available from stationery stores. Use these as a ready-made substitute for making the glue paint. Simply add your pigment.*

Makes 250 ml (8 fl oz) glue paint

Ingredients
15 g (½ oz) rabbitskin
   granules
250 ml (8 fl oz) water
1 tsp pigment (here I
   used equal quantities
   of Raw Umber and
   Titanium White) in
   solution (*see page 25*)

You will need
2 bowls, one larger than
   the other
small pot or bowl
paintbrush
night light candle

1 Soak the rabbitskin glue granules in half of the water in a bowl and leave overnight.

2 The next day add the remaining water to the mixture and stand the bowl in a larger bowl of hot water to dissolve the soaked granules. The result will be a liquid, jelly-like solution.

3 Decant a small amount of glue at a time, add pigment and then paint. Keep it warm to stop it setting by lighting a small night light candle underneath your work.

RIGHT: *This simple pattern, painted with glue paint, helps to frame this door.*

Gum arabic paint
watercolour wash

To decorate paper blinds or lampshades, a thin paint is needed so the decoration does not crack and the blind stays flexible. On a lampshade, the paintbrush marks must not be revealed when the lamp is switched on and this thin but strong binder is just the one to use. Gum arabic is normally used to make watercolour paint for use on paper. To improve on its plasticity, honey has been added in the past (*see below*).

The globules of gum dissolve easily in hot water to make a fine, sticky liquid to which the pigment is added. It can be used like watercolour paint, diluted with lots of water, or by wetting the surface first and then adding the densely coloured paint. This makes the colour spread out with a soft blurred edge. Use white pigment sparingly to keep the paint translucent – a particular characteristic of watercolour paint.

ABOVE: *Tropical acacia trees from Asia, Africa and Australia shed 'tears' of sap from their trunks which harden into globules on drying. The best quality comes from the Sudan and Senegal.*

Makes 60 ml (2 fl oz) gum arabic paint

Ingredients
15 g (½ oz) gum arabic
60 ml (2 fl oz) boiling
    water
1 tsp pigment (here I
    used Red Ochre) in
    solution (*see page 25*)

You will need
bowl
paintbrush

1 Take some 'tears' of gum arabic and crush them so they are all a similar size. Add boiling water and stir well with a paintbrush until all the gum has dissolved.

ABOVE: *Other ingredients can be added to the basic gum arabic and water to improve on its smoothness and fluidity. For example, honey and glycerine can be added to the basic gum* mixture to improve its plasticity and free-flowing qualities. For an opaque gouache paint, add dextrin (see starch paint on page 68) and chalk to the basic recipe.

OPPOSITE: *To achieve the softened effect on this blind, I painted Red Ochre and Spring Green pigments in gum arabic on a wet background. The result is a subtle blurring of colours.*

2 Add pigment in solution and use.

Fabric paint
soft & fluid

Fabric is usually coloured with dyes but it is actually very easy to paint using pigment and a binder specifically made for the job. The binder appears white when first applied, but like many of the modern water-based products it becomes transparent when dry. It is possible to mix the ingredients to any consistency use a little water to make it thin, or use more pigment to make a thicker paste. Apply the paint with a paintbrush, roller or sponge on any weight of fabric and of any colour. A pattern can be made using either stamps or a stencil or freehand.

Mixing bronze powders (*see page 39*) instead of pigments into the fabric medium results in a similar effect to pigment powder. But the bronze powders and binder need to be mixed to a more paste-like consistency than the pigments in order to show up well and to have a shine.

Printing on translucent or wide-mesh fabric means that the paint can sink through the fabric. But on textured or deep-pile fabrics the paint tends to sit on the surface, resulting in a stiffer fabric. Bear this in mind when planning your fabric painting because you might not want to be sitting next to something that is not soft to the touch but, on the other hand, a wall panel might benefit from this texture.

When painting fabric it is important to protect your work surface by laying the fabric on old newspapers. The paint is quite likely to soak through the fabric and will stain a wooden work top. After you have painted the colour on to the fabric, iron it to set the colour into the material. This can be done from the back or from the front of the fabric. But if you are ironing on the front, lay another piece of fabric between the painted surface and the iron to protect it.

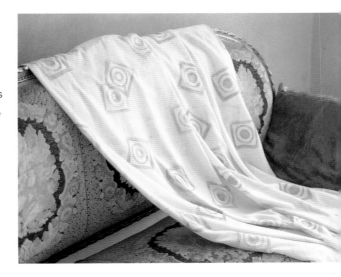

ABOVE: *An off-white, sheer fabric printed with gold bronze powder* (see page 39) *in fabric medium applied with a stamp.*

Makes 30 ml (1 fl oz) fabric paint

Ingredients
30 ml (1 fl oz) fabric medium
1 tsp pigment (here I used Hansa Yellow)
water (optional)

You will need
bowl or plate
metal spoon
bristle brush

OPPOSITE: *Thin cotton calico has been made into a colourful curtain by painting on rough rectangles of colour.*

Put some fabric binder in a bowl or on a plate and add a little of the pigment and, if necessary, water to help the consistency. Mix together and then apply with a bristle brush to the fabric. Mix a little as you go or, for colour consistency, mix a large quantity at one time, in which case mix the pigment in solution first.

Cheat's gesso
quick trick

This cheating form of gesso is inspired by the recipe on the following page and has a crude similarity with the real thing but purists will probably dislike the association being made. In comparison to real gesso, the surface is hard and unyielding when dry, and sticky when wet, but it is quick to use and easily available. It is especially good for making textures and for incising into when wet to make designs.

Cheat's gesso can be made in two ways – either add whiting to PVA glue or use a proprietary plaster filler made for filling cracks. This can be bought in powder form, in tubes or tubs. Add sufficient water to make a paste-like consistency, which can then be shaped to make designs in relief. The more water that is added to the mixture, the more possible it is to coat a surface with it.

ABOVE: *A plain pelmet has been made more interesting by being painted with a mixture of filler, water and Cobalt Blue pigment. This was then incised to reveal the white base colour.*

Makes 250 ml (8 fl oz) cheat's gesso

Ingredients
8 tbsp whiting
8 tbsp PVA glue
8 tsp pigment (here I used Cobalt Blue) in solution (*see page 25*)
OR
225 g (8 oz) proprietary filler
water (optional)
pigment as above

You will need
bowl or tray
mixing stick
knife, bristle brush or piping bag

OPPOSITE: *First, blue pigmented whiting and PVA was applied with a knife. Then proprietary plaster was applied using a piping bag to make the raised lines.*

1 Mix together the whiting and PVA glue until a stiff, paint-like consistency is achieved. Then add the pigment in solution until you have achieved your desired colour. Alternatively, mix filler with water to a similar consistency and then add the pigment.

2 Apply the mixture with a knife, bristle brush or piping bag.

Classic gesso
traditional luxury

This is not a paint but a liquid coating for wood, which dries to a smooth and absorbent but hard surface. This is a particularly superb coating for carved soft pinewood. It flows over the grain, smoothing rough edges and imperfect joins. The result is a finish that looks like moulded plaster as it obliterates the wood. It is then ready to be painted or gilded.

Classic gesso is made simply from glue, usually rabbitskin granules, and whiting or chalk, although there are many variations on these basic ingredients. The recipe is very simple but, like making bread, it requires forethought and planning to be ready when needed as the granules must soak overnight. Although your first results will be adequate, practice and attention to detail will improve the finish. Gesso can also be built up in relief designs or incised. This product can be kept in a refrigerator for a few days only.

Makes 250 ml (8 fl oz) classic gesso

Ingredients
15 g (½ oz) rabbitskin granules
250 ml (8 fl oz) water
500 g (1 lb 2 oz) whiting

You will need
2 bowls, one larger than the other
metal spoon
jam jar
sieve (optional)

OPPOSITE: *A stool made from soft pine, which has been given about five coats of gesso.*

1 Soak the rabbitskin granules in half the water overnight in a bowl. The next day, add the remaining water to the mixture and stand the bowl in a larger bowl quarter-filled with hot (not boiling) water and stir the mixture to dissolve the granules. You may need to renew the hot water once it has cooled down too much to be effective. Reserve a small amount of the resulting size in a jam jar to coat the raw wood (*see right*).

2 Slowly add the whiting to the hot liquid, stirring all the time until the mixture is the consistency of pouring cream.

3 At this stage you may choose to sieve the gesso to remove any lumps. But this is an optional refinement.

APPLYING GESSO

Dampen the wood with the reserved rabbitskin glue (*see step 1*) before applying the first coat of gesso. The first coats will dry within a few minutes but the drying time will get slower as the coats build up. Use a thin, flat varnishing brush, applying each layer in a different direction. Between four and six coats of gesso are usually necessary to create a gesso coat that is thick enough for you to be able to sandpaper the last layer a little for a total ivory-like smoothness.

Beer glaze
old-style decorating

Long ago, resourceful painters must have improvised with some left-over beer in search of a medium to 'hold' pigment. The resulting combination of sugar and alcohol is thin but viscous and because it is without colour, it fulfils the requirements of a glaze in two ways. The colour that the glaze is painted over can be seen and the glaze itself is slow drying, so allowing the decorator to work the paintbrush and refine the wood pattern.

The beer needs to be flat so that bubbles do not interfere with the work and you may prefer to mix the pigment into a small amount of beer first *(see page 25)* to avoid lumps. Make the recipe as below and then apply over a base painted a lighter colour and give it a wood effect pattern by dabbing and texturing it with paintbrushes or sponges. Once dry, varnish with a non-water-based varnish such as shellac, French polish or oil varnish.

Makes 30 ml (1 fl oz) beer glaze

Ingredients
2 tbsp flat beer
1½ tsp pigment (here
   I used Raw Sienna) in
   solution

You will need
bowl
metal spoon

OPPOSITE: *A classic 1930s-style walnut tabletop made using this recipe. Dab and pull a wide paintbrush over the base.*

LEFT: *In the past, glaze was made from gin in Holland, where it was cheap. Experiment by making glazes with other alcohols, such as the honey saki that is shown here.*

1 Pour the beer into a bowl and add enough pigment to colour the glaze but not so much that the glaze becomes opaque.

2 Mix well but take care not to make bubbles. Apply the glaze to the surface. Beginners will find it easier to do this on a horizontal surface rather then a wall as dribbles may occur.

Shellac lacquer
classic lacquer

Shellac is the material used to make the classic oriental glossy lacquer, often coloured red, terracotta or black and decorated with eastern motifs. It has long been admired for its richness of colour and its luxurious shine.

It is the oddball of all paint materials because it is the only one nowadays that is dissolved in alcohol, which means brushes are washed out in methylated spirit. Lacquer and varnish are often confused. Strictly speaking, varnish is a water- or oil-based product, unlike lacquer, which is alcohol-based and dries on evaporation of the alcohol. Used as French polish there is no colour, but used as a lacquer, pigment is added.

Applying lacquer can be tricky as it dries so quickly, but this means that achieving a high shine with many layers is easy. Leave about 20 minutes between each layer to allow the solvents to fully evaporate.

Makes 30 ml (1 fl oz) shellac lacquer

Ingredients
30 ml (1 fl oz) liquid
shellac polish
1 tsp pigment (here I
used Turquoise Blue)

You will need
bowl
paintbrush

Take the shellac polish and slowly add it to the pigment in a bowl and stir until the pigment has dissolved. Paint up to 20 layers of the colour, allowing each layer to dry before applying the next.

SHELLAC SECRETS

Shellac is a product that comes from a waxy resin created by the Indian lac insect. The females live on twigs covered with a thick coating of the lac resin. The twigs are cut and the lac melted and made into flakes. Use flakes or the liquid polish. Go for the lightest colours so your paint is not altered by the dark shellac.

ABOVE: *Shellac is a confusing material because of all the different names and forms it comes in. There are shellac flakes in various shades from golden yellow to dark brown and when it is in its liquid form it is often called French polish.*

RIGHT: *Six or seven coats of shellac mixed with Turquoise Blue pigment were coated over this shelf for a clean, neat look.*

Oil paint
rich & durable

Oil is one of the most well known paint binders, and until fairly recently was the most usual paint for both artists and house painters. There are several oils, each of which dries and hardens naturally in the air. Linseed oil is the most commonly used oil for making paints, both in its boiled and raw state. For making house-painting quality, use a boiled linseed oil as this has been heated and it has driers in it to help it be both thicker and to dry more quickly. For artist's-quality paint, raw linseed oil is used or even walnut or poppy oil. The most curious of all the qualities of oil paint is the way in which pigments absorb oil in quite different amounts. Do not be surprised when some pigments require much less than others.

LEFT: *To make an oil paint that is more like artist's paint, add as much pigment as possible so that it becomes paste-like. To further this – especially if you want to use an impasto technique – add a little beeswax. Leaving it exposed to the air or in the sun will also thicken the paint.*

RIGHT: *Here, the oil paint has been used directly on the wood as a stain-come-paint.*

Makes 250 ml (8 fl oz) oil paint

Ingredients
250 ml (8 fl oz) boiled
    linseed oil
4 tbsp pigment (here I
    used Cadmium Red)
1 tsp drier (optional)

You will need
bowl
metal spoon
paintbrush

1 Pour 2 tbsp of the boiled linseed oil into a bowl. Swirl the bowl around so that the sides are coated. Add the pigment bit by bit, continually stirring the mixture to dissolve the pigment.

2 Continue to add the pigment until it forms a cake-like consistency and drops slowly off the spoon.

3 Add more linseed oil to make a flowing medium. At this stage you can add the drier, if you choose to, which will help speed up the drying process.

PIGMENT

POWER

Mixing your own colours

The joy of making your own paint is that you have the freedom to make the exact colour you want. To do this you need to know a few basic rules so that no mistakes are made and your paint-making experiences don't end in tears.

The easiest way to start is by adding a single pigment to shop-bought white paint and on the following four pages I have given examples of my favourite colours made by simply adding different quantities of pigment powder. Of course, as I explain in the introduction to pigments (*see page 10*), the intensity of each powder varies enormously so you might well find that you need a little more or less than I have indicated here, but at least this is a starting point. Simply mix your chosen pigment powder in solution (*see page 25*) and slowly add to the paint, mixing all the while.

Making more colours

Once you have explored the possibilities of adding a single pigment to shop-bought paint – or, better still, made your own paint using one of the recipes in this book – you will feel it is time to tackle some more subtle shades. One of the truly wonderful things about pigments is that a little of this and a little of that can be added to your chosen binder to create whatever colour you want. No more small tester pots for you.

However, the often-heard lament by novice colourists is that the resulting colours are muddy and one of the main reasons for this is that too many pigments may have been mixed together so they cancel each other out.

Each of the pigments overleaf are mixed into white paint, which renders them a paler shade – for a true colour, use PVA as the base (left, above).

For this reason, it is valuable to understand how colours combine. If you have created a paint that is too bright for your living room, say, you will know how to tone it down (*see pages 96-97*). Or to enliven a colour that turns out to be too dull there are equally straightforward ways for overcoming the problem (*see pages 98-99*). Finally, I show you how to create quick and stunning colour combinations (*see pages 100-108*).

SIMPLE GUIDELINES

• Don't mix together too many pigments.

• Check the strength of a colour, as some are much stronger than others. So start with the weakest one and slowly add the stronger one. If you get the balance wrong it can result in a very different colour.

• Pigments benefit from being left wet, so to get the full strength of the colour, leave large quantities in particular for several hours and re-stir before using on your wall.

Adding pigments to white paint

Instead of buying a pre-coloured pot of paint, buy a tin of white emulsion (latex) paint and make your own colours by adding pigment. This extends your choice and gives you control. Each wall could be a different shade of the same colour by adding more of the same pigment for each wall. Alternatively, one pot of paint could be divided and used to make different colours for a room – maybe stripes on a wall. Here, the colour swatches are created by adding teaspoons of pigment to white paint, but a yellow pigment could just as easily be put into a pot of yellow or any other coloured paint.

The first thing to understand about adding pigment to white is that you will never end up with a really bright colour. Pigment in white paint results in pastel shades. If you want a bright and vibrant or a dark colour you will need to start with a clear binder such as PVA

HANSA YELLOW
(see pages 12-13)

1tsp   3tsp   6tsp

YELLOW OCHRE
(see pages 12-13)

1tsp   3tsp   6tsp

EARTH ORANGE
(see pages 12-13)

1tsp   3tsp   6tsp

EACH COLOUR IS MADE BY MIXING PIGMENT INTO 100 ML (3 FL OZ) OF WHITE PAINT

CADMIUM RED
(see pages 14-15)

1tsp   3tsp   6tsp

ALIZARIN CRIMSON
(see pages 14-15)

1tsp   3tsp   6tsp

RED OCHRE
(see pages 14-15)

1tsp   3tsp   6tsp

RAW UMBER
(see pages 20-21)

1tsp   3tsp   6tsp

or some type of glue (*see page 32*). Pigments look different in dry form and when mixed with shop-bought white emulsion (latex), a clear binder or water. Some pigment colours also change dramatically when mixed into white. Reds change from being clear and vibrant to soft and pink. Browns and earthy yellows and reds change from being plain dun colours to mellow pinks and creams.

The strength of the colour depends on what you buy. Some pigments, such as the red oxides, are very strong. These will make pinks and pale oranges. Others, such as some of the greens like Oxide of Chromium and Terre Verte, are weak and better used in delicate binders such as the two egg paints and gum arabic (*see pages 65, 66 and 74*). Remember to leave the pot of paint with your added pigment to stand for a few hours and then stir again to release any more slow-to-dissolve colour. The pigment strengths shown on these pages can only be rough guidelines.

COBALT GREEN
(see pages 18-19) 1tsp 3tsp 6tsp

VIRIDIAN
(see pages 18-19) 1tsp 3tsp 6tsp

TURQUOISE BLUE
(see pages 16-17) 1tsp 3tsp 6tsp

EACH COLOUR IS MADE BY MIXING PIGMENT INTO 100 ML (3 FL OZ) OF WHITE PAINT

PRUSSIAN BLUE
(see pages 16-17)

1tsp 3tsp 6tsp

ULTRAMARINE
(see pages 16-17)

1tsp 3tsp 6tsp

ULTRAMARINE VIOLET
(see pages 16-17)

1tsp 3tsp 6tsp

BURNT SIENNA
(see pages 14-15)

1tsp 3tsp 6tsp

Manipulating colours

It helps to know a little about how colours interact because it enables you to mix and manipulate paint colours with confidence.

All colour originates from the primary colours – red, yellow and blue. Secondary colours are made by mixing any two primary colours: blue and yellow make green; red and yellow make orange, and red and blue make purple. Colours react with each other in two basic ways: they contrast or harmonize. Looking at the colour wheel opposite, you can see that those colours that harmonize are close to each other (the adjacent colours). Those that contrast lie opposite each other (the complementary colours). So green is the complementary of red, and so on.

Complementary colours are fascinating because when juxtaposed, they enhance each other (think of scarlet cushions on a green sofa). But when mixed together they neutralize each other. This is useful to know when you are decorating a room. For instance, if you find Ultramarine too bright a blue you can tone it down with a little orange (blue's complementary) and perhaps some white. Walls painted with a grey mixed from, say, Earth Orange and Cobalt Blue (plus Titanium White, as shown below) will look good if you have orange and blue accessories in the room. Similarly, a bright red can be subtly adjusted by adding some green. Another option for dulling a jarring colour is to mix some Raw

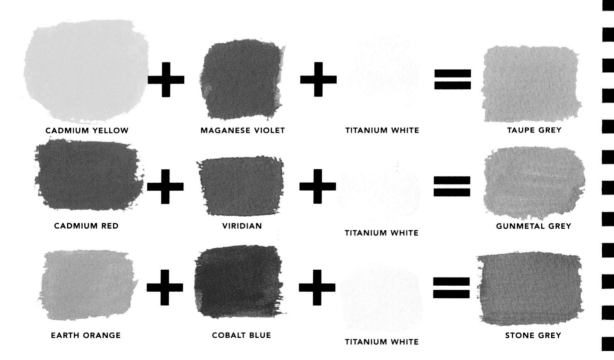

CADMIUM YELLOW	MAGANESE VIOLET	TITANIUM WHITE	TAUPE GREY
CADMIUM RED	VIRIDIAN	TITANIUM WHITE	GUNMETAL GREY
EARTH ORANGE	COBALT BLUE	TITANIUM WHITE	STONE GREY

THE VALUE OF GREY

A selection of neutral tones is the cornerstone of home decorating. Good greys are invaluable because they can be made from two complementary colours, which means they fit well in a room decorated in those colours. Here, Cadmium Yellow and Manganese Violet mixed with Titanium White make a taupe grey. Cadmium Red and Viridian are not strictly complementary but as Viridian is slightly tipped towards blue the end result (once white is added) is a gunmetal grey. And Earth Orange mixed with Cobalt Blue and white make a stone grey.

The complementary colours on the colour wheel are demonstrated here using powder pigments.

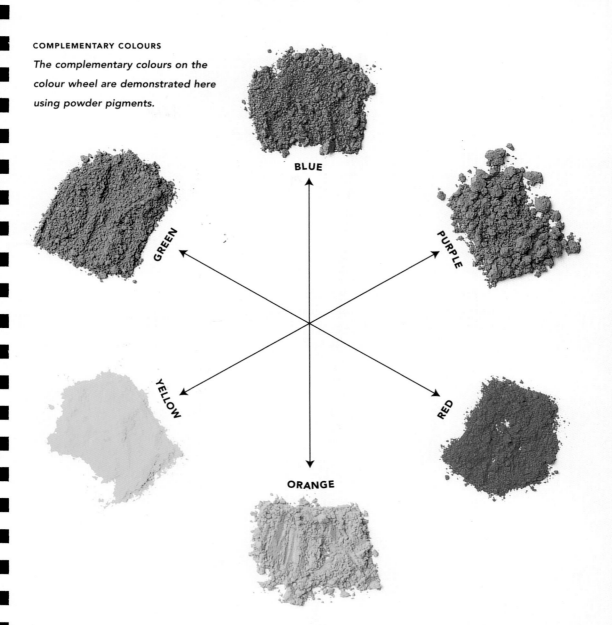

BLUE

GREEN

PURPLE

YELLOW

RED

ORANGE

ADJUSTING SHOP-BOUGHT PAINT THAT IS TOO BRIGHT

If you have bought a pot of paint that seemed just right in the shop but looks too bright on your walls, don't worry, all is not lost. The simplest approach it is to add white but remember if you have red, adding white will make your colour pink. Adding white to yellows works particularly well as it does not change the character so quickly. Try making a small swatch and adding just a small amount of white to see if it is exactly what you want. Alternatively, add the complementary colour or a little Raw Umber to tone down the colour and make it deeper. Yellow is not especially effective as a complementary colour, however, as yellow pigments tend to be weaker compared to other colours.

Umber into it. This brown has a fairly low strength so is easy to mix.

If you have a colour that looks a little dull, the easiest way to enrich it is by adding a little of its adjacent colour. For example, a red can be made warmer and more lively by adding orange to it, or darkened and enriched by adding a little purple.

In theory, this is a simple way of changing a colour but the difficulty can be in identifying the colour in the first place so that the correct adjacent colour can be added. It is obvious that a colour is red, blue or yellow, but if you want to keep very clean tones then it is as well to know the properties of your colour. For instance, if you are adding purple to a blue, know that your blue is a mid- or warm blue to begin with and not a greenish blue. For example, Prussian Blue is tinged with green, so adding purple to it will result in a more complex, perhaps too dirty, colour.

To enrich a yellow that suddenly looks insipid in your kitchen, add some orange such as Earth Orange to make it more buttery. For a more acidic yellow try a green pigment such as Cobalt Green. Keep notes of how much pigment you have added and test the colour as you go.

The adjacent colours for blue are purple and green. Because of the slightly red hue in Ultramarine, deepen it by adding a little reddish violet. The greenish aspect of Cobalt Blue can be intensified by adding more green, specifically one that is a little bluish like Viridian.

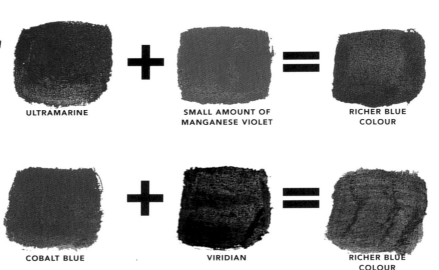

ULTRAMARINE + SMALL AMOUNT OF MANGANESE VIOLET = RICHER BLUE COLOUR

COBALT BLUE + VIRIDIAN = RICHER BLUE COLOUR

ADJUSTING SHOP-BOUGHT PAINT THAT IS TOO DULL

If your pot of paint needs to have more brilliance and intensity, this is more difficult to remedy, especially if the colour is quite deep. Unless it says otherwise, there is likely to be a lot of black in a shop-bought paint's make-up. But all is not lost because clear strong pigments can be added to give it some life. Choose strong pigments that may override the black. It is no good adding a yellow pigment as it is likely to have little effect. But the Red Oxides, some Ultramarine Blues and some Phthalocyanines are strong enough to counteract the black.

On either side of the three primaries,
red, blue and yellow, lie their secondary
mixes – or adjacent colours.

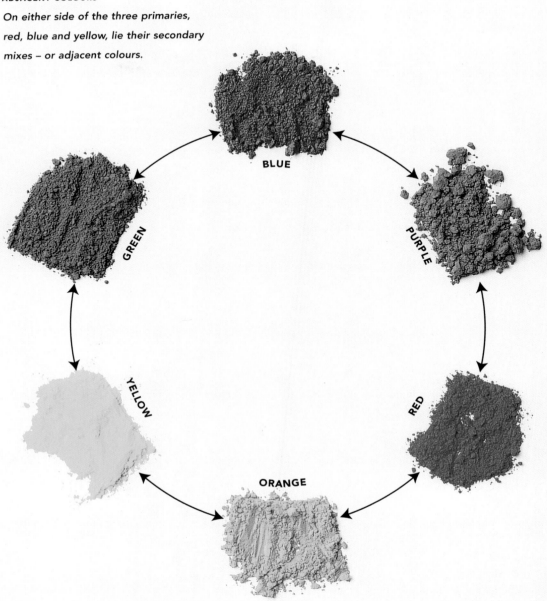

BLUE

PURPLE

GREEN

RED

YELLOW

ORANGE

ADJUSTING SHOP-BOUGHT PAINT THAT IS TOO PALE

This is the easiest problem to remedy as it is merely a question of adding more pigment to beef up the colour quantity. If a colour is too pale, it has too much white in it so remedying this is simply a matter of adding the pigment you want to be more apparent. For example, that strawberry pink you have bought for your bedroom looks so washed out at home. What to do? Add some Cadmium Red or Red Ochre. Another way to enrich the colour is to add some of the adjacent colour. So if you have a pale green or a pale blue try adding a little Prussian Blue.

Making the perfect yellow for your home

To make a brilliant, buttery yellow like that on the walls of this room on the left, you will need a strong yellow such as Hansa Yellow. Yellows are very popular for decorating interiors: bright yellows bring the sunshine, in making a cheery environment; earthy yellows make an undemanding mellow backdrop. Use the spice turmeric to make an exotic golden yellow. Avoid using a greenish lemony acidic yellow, especially in a room with little natural light. At night the yellow of the electric light will be drowned, leaving just the green. A solid acid yellow is also not such a pleasant colour to live with. Yellow pigments have little strength, so when mixing different colours, start with the yellow and add to it bit by bit.

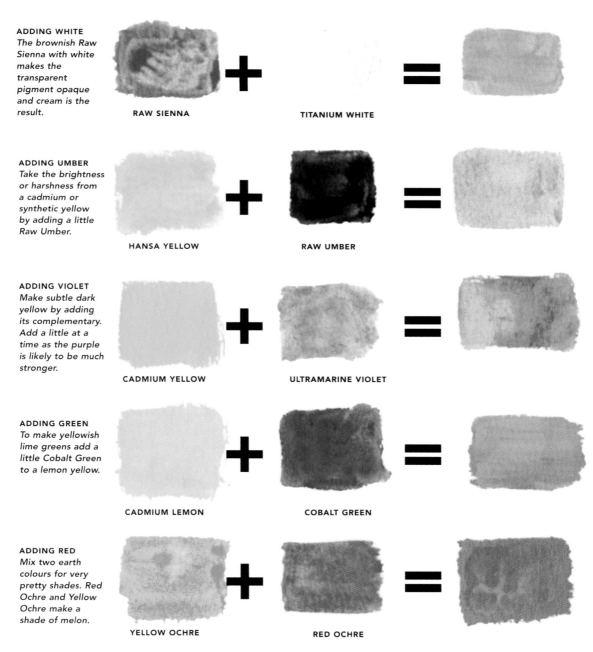

ADDING WHITE
The brownish Raw Sienna with white makes the transparent pigment opaque and cream is the result.

RAW SIENNA + TITANIUM WHITE =

ADDING UMBER
Take the brightness or harshness from a cadmium or synthetic yellow by adding a little Raw Umber.

HANSA YELLOW + RAW UMBER =

ADDING VIOLET
Make subtle dark yellow by adding its complementary. Add a little at a time as the purple is likely to be much stronger.

CADMIUM YELLOW + ULTRAMARINE VIOLET =

ADDING GREEN
To make yellowish lime greens add a little Cobalt Green to a lemon yellow.

CADMIUM LEMON + COBALT GREEN =

ADDING RED
Mix two earth colours for very pretty shades. Red Ochre and Yellow Ochre make a shade of melon.

YELLOW OCHRE + RED OCHRE =

More information on these pigments can be found on pages 12-21.

The hotter interior

In interior decoration, red can make a statement, even in small quantities. To make these rich, warm but soft reds, use the earthy terracottas such as Red Ochre enriched with Cadmium Red. The reds change most with the addition of white, making pinks. Those that are the easiest to live with are the mellow pinks made from the red earths rather than the sweet baby and strawberry pinks made using the bright clear reds or the crimson reds. The earth and Alizarin Reds are quite strong so add a little at a time. As red is a primary colour it is important to have a collection to work with to make oranges, pinks and purples. Add blues to reds for purples and add yellows to reds for oranges.

ADDING WHITE
Explore mixes of earth reds with white to see the different subtle tones of old earthy and dusty pinks, each with its own character.

VENETIAN RED   TITANIUM WHITE

ADDING UMBER
When Cadmium Red is too sharp, tone it down with a little Raw Umber and perhaps some white to bring out the colour.

CADMIUM
VERMILLION HUE   RAW UMBER

ADDING GREEN
To make a more intense red of an orange red, add a little bluish green. These two colours are similar in strength but it is best to add a little at a time.

CADMIUM
VERMILLION HUE   VIRIDIAN

ADDING YELLOW
For a clear orange do not add lemon yellow or a crimson red (any green or blue tinge makes a dirty orange). Instead, use these colours.

CADMIUM
VERMILLION HUE   CADMIUM YELLOW

ADDING RED
To make rich mahogany reds use a warm earth colour and a dark red. With white added luscious melon pinks can be made.

RED OCHRE   CADMIUM RED DARK

More information on these pigments can be found on pages 12-21.

Blue needn't mean cool

A blue bathroom can be a deeply calming place in which to relax. For this particular bathroom I used Ultramarine in the limewash recipe on page 50. On the whole, blues are very strong pigments so use a little at first to judge the strength. To make pale blue it is best to start with white and add the blue. Similarly, if you are making a pale green by mixing a blue and yellow start with the yellow and white and add the blue. For a richer blue, add either an earthy orange such as Burnt Sienna or a clearer orange such as Cadmium Orange, blue's complementary colour (*see page 96*). The blue is likely to be stronger than the orange so more of the orange will be needed to equal the blue in strength.

ADDING WHITE
This blue is so strong it is best to start with white and add the blue until the exact tone of this cool pale blue is reached.

 **PRUSSIAN BLUE** + **TITANIUM WHITE**  =

ADDING UMBER
To deepen Turquoise Blue and remove any hint of harshness, add a little Raw Umber.

 **TURQUOISE BLUE** + **RAW UMBER**  =

ADDING ORANGE
To make a more sophisticated regal blue, add either Earth Orange or Burnt Sienna to Cobalt Blue.

 **COBALT BLUE** + **EARTH ORANGE**  =

ADDING RED
These two colours make a good purple, which becomes particularly apparent when a little white is added.

 **ULTRAMARINE** + **ALIZARIN CRIMSON**  =

ADDING YELLOW
Adding the greenish Cadmium Lemon to Cobalt Blue or any greenish blue makes sage green.

 **COBALT BLUE** + **CADMIUM LEMON**  =

More information on these pigments can be found on pages 12-21.

From lime to sage green

What could be more welcoming in a hallway than green – introducing the colour of the outside world indoors. A similar colour to the wall on the left could be achieved by using Phthalocyanine Green and Burnt Sienna in PVA (*see page 32*). Roll it on using a hairy roller over a brighter green made with Cobalt Green, Hansa Yellow and a little white.

As there are fewer green pigments readily available it is often necessary to make your own greens or adjust the pigments. Adding white makes a good assortment of pale greens ranging from sage to aquamarine. To make lime green, start with a lemon yellow then add a green without any blue, such as a yellowish Phthalocyanine or Cobalt Green.

ADDING WHITE
Mixing white into any colour brings out the true nature of a pigment. Here the colour appears as a mellow mid-tone green.

 **COBALT GREEN** +  **TITANIUM WHITE** =

ADDING UMBER
Add Burnt or Raw Umber to Viridian or Phthalocyanine Green and sumptuous dark forest greens result.

 **VIRIDIAN** +  **RAW UMBER** =

ADDING RED
Viridian and Phthalocyanine green can be a little too sharp and raw. A good way to knock them back is to add some red.

 **VIRIDIAN** + **ALIZARIN CRIMSON** =

ADDING RED
To make olive green add a little Burnt Sienna and perhaps a little white to Phthalocyanine Green.

 **PHTHALOCYANINE GREEN** + **BURNT SIENNA** =

ADDING YELLOW
It is important to start with a lemony Cadmium Yellow for this mixture to make a clean bright middle green.

 **VIRIDIAN** +  **CADMIUM YELLOW** =

More information on these pigments can be found on pages 12-21.

Resource Directory

United Kingdom

ANNIE SLOAN – PRACTICAL STYLE
117 London Road
Oxford
OX3 9HZ
Tel: 01870 0082 (mail order)
Tel: 01865 768666 for local stockists
E-mail: shop@aniesloan.com
Website: www.aniesloan.com
(Kremer pigments, lustres and bronze
powders, wax, varnish, brushes,
paints and polished plaster as well as
interior decorating problems)

ATLANTIS
7-9 Plumber's Row
London E1 1EQ
Tel: 020 7377 8855
(Paints and pigments)

BAILEY PAINTS
Griffin Mill Estate
London Road
New Stroud
Thrupp
Gloucestershire
GL5 2AZ
Tel: 01453 882237
(Paints and pigments)

BAILEY PLASTERS
Wtareside Studios
99 Rotherhithe Street
London SE16 4NF
Tel: 020 731 9049
(Ready coloured and uncoloured
plasters. Commissions undertaken)

BRODIE AND MIDDLETON
68 Dury Lane
London WC2 B 5SP
Tel: 020 7836 3289

CREATIVE DECORATING
Marantha
Whitbrook
Wadebridge
Cornwall
PL27 7ED
Tel: 01208 814528

L. CORNELISSEN AND SON LTD
105 Great Russell Street
London WC1B 3RY
Tel: 020 7636 1045
Fax: 020 7636 3655
E-mail: info@cornelissen.com

A P FITZPATRICK
142 Cambridge Heath Road
Bethnal Green Road
London E1 5QJ
Tel: 020 7790 0085
E-mail: APFColours@aol.com
(Suppliers of Kremer Pigments,
Lascaux Colours and a
comprehensive range of
high quality artist's materials. Shop,
catalogue and full mail-order service)

SARAH HOLCOMBE
Studio 3
Cornwell House
21 Clerkenwell Green
London EC1R 0DX,
Tel: 020 7251 6631
E-mail: SHocombe@aol.com
(Fresco painter interested in bringing
contemporary fresco to a wider
audience. See pages 54-55.
Undertakes mural and fresco
commissions)

FRANCIS ILES ARTWORKS
104 High Street
Rochester
ME1 1JT
Tel: 01634 843881
Website: www.artycat.com

LONDON GRAPHIC CENTRE
16-18 Shelton Street
Covent Garden
London WC2 9JJ
Tel: 020 7240 0095
(Paints and pigments)

MILLER'S ART SHOP
28 Stockwell Street
Glasgow
GI 4RT
Tel: 0141 553 1660
Email: info @millers-art.co.uk
(Artist's paints and pigments)

KARIN MOORHOUSE INTERIORS
26 High Street
Arundel
Sussex
BN18 9AB
Tel: 01903 884367
(Paints as well as pigments, waxes,
varnishes, etc.)

PAINT AND PAPER LTD
11 Hellesdon Park Industrial Estate
Drayton Road
Norwich
Norfolk
NR6 5DR
Tel: 01603 400777
(Paints and pigments)

RELICS OF WITNEY
35 Bridge Street
Witney
Oxon
OX8 6DA
Tel: 01993 704611
(Paints and pigments)

SERENDIPITY
12 Devonshire Street
Penrith
Cumbria
CA11 7SR
Tel: 01768 895977
(Paints and pigments)

THE STENCIL SHOP
Eyam Hall Craft Centre
Eyam
Hope Valley
Derbyshire
S32 5QW
Tel: 01433 639001

STUART STEVENSON
68 Clerkenwell Road,
London EC1 5QA
Tel: 020 7253 1693
Fax: 020 749 00451
(Artist's supplier of pigments, resins,
gums and other traditional binders)

WEBBS OF TENTERDEN
51 High Street
Tenterden
Kent
TN30 6BH
Tel: 01580 762132
(Paints and pigments)

WRIGHTS OF LYMM LTD
Millers Lane
Lymm
Cheshire
WA13 9RG
(Paints and pigments)

USA and Canada

BEST LIEBCO CORPORATION
1201 Jackson Street
Philedelphia
Pennsylvania 19148
Toll-free: 1-800-523-9095
Fax: (215) 463-0988
Email: bestliebco@aol.com

THE BRITISH & COLUMBIAN TRADING COMPANY
110 Ponderosa Avenue
Kaleden, B.C. V0H 1K0
Canada
Tel: 1-250-497-6871
Fax: 1-250-497-6891
Website: www.bctradingco.com
(Showroom with Annie Sloan Paints, pigments etc.)

BRIWAX WOODCARE PRODUCTS
220 South Main Street
Auburn, Maine 04210
Toll-free: 1-800-274-9299
Fax: (212) 504 9550
Email: information@BriwaxWoodcare.com
Website: www.BriwaxWoodcare.com

GOLDEN ARTISTS COLORS, INC
188 Bell Road
New Berlin, New York 13411-9527
Toll-free: 1-888-397-2468
Tel: (607) 847-6154
Fax: (607) 847-6767
E-mail: orderlineinfo@goldenpaints.com
Website: www.goldenpaints.com

HK HOLBEIN
Box 555, 20 Commerce Street
Williston, Vermont 05495
Toll-free: 1-800-682-6686
Tel: (802) 862-4573
Fax: (802) 658-5889
Website: www.holbeinhk.com

HOMESTEAD HOUSE AUTHENTIC MILK PAINT
95 Niagara Street
Toronto, Ontario M5V 1C3
Tel: (416) 504 9984

KAMA PIGMENTS
85 Jean Talon Ouest, #4
Montreal
Quebec
Canada
H2R 2WB
Tel/fax: 1-514-272-2173
Website: www.kamapigment.com
(Retail, mail order and Internet service in both French and English)

KREMER PIGMENTS INC.
228 Elizabeth Street
New York, NY 10012
Tel: (800) 995 5501
Fax: (212) 219 2395
E-mail: kremerinc@aol.com
Website: www.kremer-pigmente.com
Hours: Mon - Sat 11 - 6:30 E.T.

PAINTERS AND DECORATING RETAILERS ASSOCIATION
403 Axminister Drive
St. Louis, Missouri 63026-2941
Tel: (636) 326-2636
Fax: (636) 326-1823
Website: www.pdra.org

PAINT EFFECTS
2426 Fillmore Street
San Francisco, Calfornia 94115
Tel: (415) 292-7780
Fax: (415) 292-7782
Website: www.painteffects.com

PARIS PAINT TECHNIQUES
Valerie Traynor
91 Rutland Street
Carlisle, Massachusetts 01741
Te:l (978) 369-3440
E-mail: paristrayn@aol.com

PEARL PAINTS
308 Canal Street
New York, New York 10013
Toll-free: 1-800 221-6845 x2297
Tel: (212) 431-7932 x2297
Website: www.pearlpaint.com

PERIWINKLE ESSENTIAL STENCILS
P.O. Box 457
West Kennebunk, Maine 04094
Tel: (207) 985-8020
Fax: (207) 985-1601
E-mail: periwinkle@cybertours.com
Website: www.cybertours.com/periwinkle/home.html

PIERRE FINKELSTEIN INSTITUTE OF DECOARTIVE PAINTING, INC.
20 West 20th Street, Suite 1009
New York, New York 10011
Toll-free: 1-888-328-9278
Website: www.pfinkelstein.com

R&F HANDMADE PAINTS, INC.
110 Prince Street
Kingston, New York 12401
Toll-free: 1-800-206-8088
Tel: (914) 331-3112
Fax: (914) 331-3242
E-mail: mail@RFPaints.com
Website: www.rfpaints.com

SEPP LEAF PRODUCTS, INC
381 Park Avenue South
New York, New York 10016
Toll-free: 1-800-971-7377
Tel: (212) 683-2840
Fax: (212) 725-0308
E-mail: sales@seppleaf.com
Website: www.seppleaf.com

SHARON MATAS
309 Earles Lane
Newton Square, Philadelphia 19073
Tel: (610) 396-4952

SINOPIA PIGMENTS & MATERIALS
3385 22nd Street
San Francisco, CA 94110
Tel: (415) 824-3180
Fax: (415) 824-3280
E-mail: pigments@sinopia.com
Website: www.sinopia.com
(Pigments, traditional and modern binders, gold and composition leaf, decorative and lime paint. Mail order.)

STAMPERS STUDIO
2255A Queen Street East
Toronto, Ontario
Tel: (416) 690-4446
Fax: (416) 690-7131
Website: www.the-beaches.com/stampers

SURFACE SOLUTIONS
2018 Ranleigh Avenue
Toronto, Ontario M4N 1W9
Tel: (416) 488-6404

Australia

PORTER'S ORIGINAL PAINTS
Sydney, Australia
Tel: (818) 623-9394
Fax: (818) 623-9210
Website: www.porters.com.au

Index

Acknowledgments

Dedicated to Jane Warnick and Kathy Moss - practical and stylish!

Particular thanks to Sarah Holcombe for help with the frescos and Philip Bailey for the plaster work. Thanks also to Alan Fitzpatrick for help with pigment information and to Corinne at Brodie and Middleton. I thank also Andrew Townsend for the use of his delightful limewashed bathroom on page 104. Special painting and making help was given by Charlotte le Poivedin and I thank everybody at practical style for their support, including Justin Earl. Medals for valiant effort should also be awarded to Emma Callery, Luise Roberts and Tino Tedaldi for getting this book out under terrific difficulties.

Page 3: untitled drawing by Annie Sloan.
All the following products came from Annie Sloan - practical style:
page 31, chair by Trannon; page 33, print entitled 'Flashback' by Jo Melvin;
pages 34 and 35, fluffy lamp and noodle bowls; page 41, silk cushions from a selection;
page 51, from the Swedish Chair company; page 60, Hacienda chair and cushion;
page 65, yellow bowl from a selection; page 81, French-style stool;
page 83, egg cups from a selction of wire designs.